THE C...
AND LOVE

A Treatise on the Love of Christ for the People of God

Sister Marie Celeste, S.C.

University Press of America,® Inc.
Lanham • New York • Oxford

Copyright © 1998
Sister Marie Celeste, S.C.

University Press of America,® Inc.
4720 Boston Way
Lanham, Maryland 20706

12 Hid's Copse Rd.
Cummor Hill, Oxford OX2 9JJ

Library of Congress Cataloging-in-Publication Data

Marie Celeste, Sister, S.C.
The church and love : a treatise on the love of Christ for the people
of God / Sister Marie Celeste, S. C.
p.   cm.
l. Sacred Heart, Devotion to. 2. Church.   I. Title.
BX2157.M335 1998   232—dc21   98-17863 CIP

ISBN 0-7618-1131-1 (cloth: alk. ppr.)
ISBN 0-7618-1132-X (pbk: alk. ppr.)

⊖™ The paper used in this publication meet the minimum
requirements of American National Standard for information
Sciences—Permanence of Paper for Printed Library Materials,
ANSI Z39.48—1984

Joannes Paulus PP. II

*"The Heart of the World
is caught in the
descending radiance
of the Heart of God."*

Chardin

Nihil Obstat

Monsignor Thomas E. Madden, D.D.

Censor Librorum

Altoona-Johnstown Diocese

1971

Imprimatur

† James J. Hogan

Bishop of Altoona-Johnstown Diocese

CONTENTS

PART I

PART II

ACKNOWLEDGEMENTS

I should like to express again my gratitude to my community, the Seton Hill Sisters of Charity; and to my family for their moral support in this work; to the Reverend Francis Larkin, SS.CC., National Director of the Enthronement of the Sacred Heart who requested the English translation; to the late Very Reverend B. U. Fay, O.P., and to the late Reverend Joseph F. Hogan, S.J., former Director of the Apostleship of Prayer of the Sacred Heart of Jesus; to the Most Reverend James J. Hogan, Bishop of the Altoona-Johnstown diocese for the Imprimatur; to Monsignor Thomas E. Madden, D.D., Censor Librorum, Altoona-Johnstown Diocese; to Brother Aloysius Milella, S.S.P., for the Foreword of this book; to the James D. Cuzzolina Family and Paul E. Schreiner Family; to Joyce Dinello, Printing Services and Alfredo Perez, Copy Center, Loyola University Chicago; and to Mrs. Natalie F. Hector, Computer Typist.

In addition, my deep appreciation extends to the
following benefactors for their continued interest in my
publications: Reverend Gerald L. Brown, United States
Provincial for the Society of Saint Sulpice, Reverend Yves
Danjou, C.M., Provincial of the Congregation of the
Mission, Paris, France; His Eminence Joseph Cardinal
Bernardin, Archdiocese of Chicago; Reverend Monsignor
Robert A. Brucato, Chancellor, Archdiocese of New York;
Most Reverend J. Faber MacDonald, Bishop of Grand
Falls/Windsor, Newfoundland, Canada; Monsignor Jean
Honoré, Archbishop of Tours, France; Archbishop
Pasquale Macchi, Archbishop of <u>Loreto</u>, Italy; Abbot
David J. Cyr, O.S.B., Marmion Abbey, Aurora, Illinois;
Brother Aloysius Milella, S.S.P., former Superior and
Editor-in-Chief, Alba House Press, Staten Island, New
York; Reverend Robert P. Maloney, C.M., Superior
General of the Congregation of the Mission, Rome, Italy;
Most Reverend Harry J. Flynn, Archibishop of St.
Paul/Minneapolis; Reverend Anselm Romb, O.F.M.
Conv., former Editor of Marytown Press, Libertyville,
Illinois; Monsignor Hugh J. Phillips, Chaplain, National

Shrine Grotto of Lourdes, Emmitsburg, Maryland;
Reverend Monsignor Joseph M. O'Toole, Altoona/
Johnstown diocese; and Doctor Gerald W. McCulloh,
Department of Theology, Loyola University Chicago.

Sister Marie Celeste, S.C.
Seton Hill, Pennsylvania
Loyola University Chicago

February 7, 1996

FOREWORD

In keeping with its basic scope of bringing the Church to renewal through a sharper re-focusing of its Christ-centered life, Vatican II proposed fresh forms and expression to time honored devotional practices.

Over the centuries, few practices achieved the spontaneous and particular veneration given the Heart of Christ. Historically rooted in the piercing climax of Cavalry, it claimed the attention of mystics and Christian writers of the earliest ages. So enamored and taken by the unsparing self-spending of the Crucified Redeemer, St. Paul devotedly exclaimed that nothing could ever separate him from the sustaining love of Christ.

Over the centuries, too, few devotional practices maintained a theological soundness, relevancy and staying power as that to the Sacred Heart of Jesus. As this admirable treatise affirms, devotion to the Heart of Christ has been a historical and liturgical constant because fundamentally it is the discovery (and rediscovery) that the Lord loves us. So it has rung with immediacy of appeal to every category of persons whatever the epoch, times or extenuating circumstances.

In commenting on the invocations of the Litany of the Sacred Heart, Pope John Paul II observed: "Through this Heart, the humanity of Christ is in a particular way the 'temple of God' and at the same time, through this Heart, it remains open to man and to everything human: 'Heart of Jesus, of whose fullness we have all received'."

In our world of idolized self-sufficiency and self-centeredness, but as well of pitiful brokenness and utter inhumanity, the invitation of the Master that originally stirred so much hope and healing may be heeded again to our immense benefit: "Come to Me. Learn of Me, for I am meek and humble of Heart."

This is the yearning and premise of this timeless treatise. Its re-issue cannot but be happily recommended.

Brother Aloysius Milella, S.S.P.
Past Editor-in-Chief of Alba House
Publishers, Staten Island, New York

Feast of the Ascension of Christ,
May 16, 1998

PREFACE

The Church and Love: A Treatise on the Love of Christ for the People of God reveals once again God's constant care of mankind. This treatise is an appeal to God's people to re-animate and enliven the time-honored devotion to the Sacred Heart of Jesus in compliance with His Holiness Pope John Paul II for *Jubilee 2000*. In the words of Christ Himself in the Upper Room where He had gathered with His Apostles at the Last Supper and instituted the Eucharist, the Sacrament of His love, He prayed for them and spoke these words: "So that your love for me may live in them" (His people) (Jn 17-26).

In this era of Christianity and Ecumenism, this message appears now more timely than ever in the history of mankind. Embracing all nations, it sheds light on "the way, the truth and the life" (Jn 14:6) to eternal peace and happiness.

Divided into two parts, Part I of this work is an effort to document the love of the Sacred Heart of Jesus for God's people, which I translated from the French: *Vatican*

II and the Cult of the Sacred Heart of Jesus by Rev. Jean Ladame, Superior of the Chaplains at Paray-le-Monial, France, and published by the Franciscan Publishers, Pulaski, Wisconsin 1972. An authoritative document, the master work should dispel once and for all the fears and doubts of the faithful concerned about the place of this devotion in the Church today.

Based on Holy Scripture and the writings of the early Fathers and Doctors of the Church, this devotion, as we have noted, had its origin at the Last Supper of Christ with His Apostles, and at the passion of Christ on Calvary, when Longinus, the soldier, pierced Christ's Heart with a lance, causing Him to shed His last drop of blood for the salvation of mankind. Having survived the Ages, it is as old as the Church herself.

The private revelations of the mystics of the Middle Ages, and the lives of the Saints, namely, Bernard of Clairvaux, Catherine of Siena, John Eudes, Margaret Mary, all attest to the authenticity of Christ's love for His people symbolized by His heart.

In 1964, Pope Paul VI, in promulgating the *Documents of Vatican Council II*, affirmed that these documents "bring to light the ineffable mystery of the Church... that sprang from the mind and heart of God" of which the Sacred Heart of Jesus is the clear symbol. Thus, they embody the various aspects of the Church's doctrines, teachings and practices, such as, the *Sacred Liturgy*; *Religious Life*; *Laity*; *Education*; the *Blessed Virgin Mary*, to name only a few, all embracing the *Sacred Heart of Jesus*.

In translating this work, I used *The New Jerusalem Bible*, 1966, 1985, 1990 edition, for all biblical references, and adhered closely to the English translations of *The Documents of Vatican II* by Walter M. Abbott, S.J., and Very Rev. Msgr. Joseph Gallagher for the quotations cited therein. When referring to the Council documents in quoting from them, I used the abbreviated titles.

* * *

Part II, a timely Epilogue which complements the account on the historical documents of Vatican Council II and the devotion of the Sacred Heart of Jesus, was inspired by His Holiness Pope John Paul II and his plan to commemorate the second millennium of the birth of Christ during the *Jubilee Year 2000*. Stemming from his youth and continuing through his pontificate to the present, Pope John Paul II's devotion to the Sacred Heart of Jesus never faltered. To propagate this devotion among the people of God, he focused his "Sunday Angelus messages" on the Litany of the Sacred Heart of Jesus.

Documentation for this epilogue was taken from his own writings and preaching: *The Angelus Meditations on the Litany of the Sacred Heart of Jesus*; the account of his visit to Paray-le-Monial on the occasion of the third centenary of the death of Saint Margaret Mary Alacoque, whose life story has propagated this devotion since the seventeenth century when she was canonized.

Documentation on Saint Claude La Colombière, friend and spiritual director of Saint Margaret Mary, was taken from the homily of His Holiness John Paul II at the Canonization Mass of Saint Claude La Colombière, May 31, 1992. The account was published in the *Osservatore Romano*, June 3, 1992.

In my labor of love in the church, it is my ardent desire that all God's People, in recompense for God's love, will take to heart this devotion *to establish peace throughout the world* and draw ever closer to the Sacred Heart of Jesus.

February 7, 1996

Sister Marie Celeste, S.C.
Seton Hill, Pennsylvania
Loyola University Chicago

ABBREVIATED TITLES OF THE DOCUMENTS OF VATICAN II QUOTED IN THE CHURCH AND LOVE

THE CHURCH

>   (Dogmatic Constitution on the Church)

LITURGY

>   (Constitution on the Sacred Liturgy)

THE CHURCH TODAY

>   (Pastoral Constitution on the Church
>   in the Modern World)

COMMUNICATIONS

>   (Decree on the Instruments of Social
>   Communication)

ECUMENISM

>   (Decree on Ecumenism)

RELIGIOUS LIFE

>   (Decree on the Appropriate Renewal
>   of the Religious Life)

LAITY

>   (Decree on the Apostolate of the Laity)

PART I

CHAPTER ONE

THE BIRTH OF THE CHURCH

In keeping with the wishes of the Popes who convoked Vatican Council II and convened its sessions, and through the efforts and the concern of the Bishops assembled there, the twenty-first ecumenical council of the church set out to be pre-eminently pastoral. No anathemas were pronounced nor were there any condemnations of heretical doctrines and no new dogmas were defined. There was only the question of the spiritual renewal of the People of God in the teachings of our Savior Jesus Christ in the Church He founded, and a practical adaptation of this Church, timeless by its very nature, to today's world.

The work of the *aggiornamento*, however, required an exact and well defined understanding of the essence and functions of the Church. Its doctrines were studied in depth by the Council Fathers, and on November 21, 1964,

Pope Paul VI promulgated the *Dogmatic Constitution on the Church*, which stated that the doctrinal work of the Ecumenical Council Vatican II was completed. The mystery of the Church had been examined and studied, and the basic doctrines of its divine origin were drawn up.

In presenting this constitution to the People of God, the bishops said: "We consider it the cornerstone of Vatican Council II and of our apostolic work for years to come. Indeed, the times required that we tell the modern world what the Church is and what it wishes to be. We cannot enter into dialogue with the world of today until we know what we are in Christ."

Summarizing in one sentence the entire context of this constitution, the bishops added: "The Church, that is offering itself to us today, is the same Church that sprang from the mind and heart of God."

In his letter of May 25, 1965, Pope Paul VI expressed himself in like manner: "Vatican Council II," he affirmed, "has brought to light the ineffable mystery of the Church." But this mystery, our Holy Father specifically states, can only be well understood when we consider carefully the eternal love of the Incarnate Word, of which the Sacred Heart of Jesus is the clear symbol. In *The Church* (3), we read: "The Church, or, in other words, the Kingdom of Christ now present in mystery, grows visibly in the world through the power of God. This inauguration and this growth are both symbolized by the blood and water which flowed from the open side of the crucified Jesus" (Jn. 19:34).

Indeed, the Church was born and takes its nourishment from the opened side and the pierced Heart of Christ, the Redeemer, for Christ sacrificed Himself for her to make her holy, "cleansing her in the bath of water with a form of words" (Eph. 5:25-26).

In order to be faithful to the teachings of Vatican Council II, Christians must meditate on the mystery of the Church, penetrate its depths, and live the demands of a holy life. From the heart of Christ that gave it birth, they must discover and understand more deeply what the Church is. On Calvary with Our Lady and Saint John who witnessed the stroke of Longinus' lance that pierced Christ's side, the mystery of the Church was revealed to all Christians. As St. Paul says: "Only now, through the Church we learn how comprehensive God's wisdom really is; it is exactly according to the plan which He had from all eternity in Christ Jesus our Lord" (Eph. 3:11).

This mystery that Saint Paul was given to know is the mystery of Christ, the mystery of the Church. For as he tells us: "It means that Gentiles now share the same inheritance, that they are part of the same body, and that the same Promise has been made to them in Christ Jesus, through the Gospel" (Eph. 3:6). "To penetrate such a mystery is by the very fact to know the love of Christ which is beyond all knowledge" (Eph. 3:19). In a word, to discover the Church is to discover the Heart of Christ.

*　*　*　*　*

In his *History of the Devotion to the Sacred Heart*, Father Hamon, a French priest, wrote these surprising lines: "Devotion to the Sacred Heart, one might say, was almost nothing prior to 1290," that is, before the time of Saint Gertrude and Saint Mechtilda. If one calls devotion to the Sacred Heart a mystical and personal experience, the falling in love of a saintly soul, a familiarity with the love of Christ, Father Hamon is undoubtedly correct.

But is this the only authentic devotion to the Sacred Heart? One should not deny all that religion, the cult and attachment to God demand of Christians individually, neither should one omit the communal or collective aspects of religious actions. Both forms of devotion are needed and complement each other, since the Church is a society of persons. In speaking of the love of Christ in the redemption, St. Paul used two parallel and correlative formulas: "He loved me and sacrificed himself for my sake!" (Gal. 2:20). "Christ loved the Church and sacrificed himself for her" (Eph. 5:25).

Where, then, came the two-fold contemplation of the open side of Jesus Christ? With many of the mystics, namely, Mechtilda, Catherine of Siena, Bernard of Clairvaux, and others, the devotion was private and personal, an exchange of hearts, the openness of a loving heart to the wounded Heart of Christ.

This aspect, according to the lives of the saints, has flourished since the thirteenth century. But previous to that time, the Fathers of the Church had already established devotion to the pierced Heart of Christ. When they commented on the creation of Eve, the door of Noah's Ark or the Canticle of Canticles in the Old Testament, especially the "you have wounded my heart," they instituted the true devotion to the Heart of Christ in the Church. Thus, it was not with Saint Gertrude that devotion to the Sacred Heart was born, but with Holy Scripture itself and tradition which revealed the love of Christ for his Churoh.

This devotion began to appear again in a personal and mystical way in the seventeenth century with Saint John Eudes and Saint Margaret Mary. In fact, Saint John Eudes became its promoter by composing a Mass and an Office in its honor, the liturgy being the expression of piety not of an individual person, but of a Christian community. Saint Margaret Mary and her followers requested that a universal feast for the Heart of Christ be established in public reparation for the sins of mankind.

Now, at a time when again the mystery of the Church is revealed to all men, we must return to the historical and liturgical aspects of this devotion. This does not mean one must abandon, or prohibit personal devotion. This devotion today must take its source and inspiration both from the mystics and tradition, and from the thinking of the Christian writers of the early ages.

What then is the teaching of the Church on the

devotion to the Sacred Heart of Jesus? First, that the Church sprang from this Heart. "For the early Fathers," writes Cardinal Lercaro, "the stroke of Longinus' spear opening the side of Christ represents the greatest symbol of the founding of the Church as related in the Gospel of Saint John--'the Pentecost of the Crucified'." (Cf. Ladame, p. 3, *Vatican II and the Cult of the Sacred Heart*). In this mystery of the passion, the birth of the new Church was accomplished. From it flow two fundamental sacraments, Baptism and the Holy Eucharist, both signs and means of the fruitfulness and ministry of holy Mother the Church. Through them, she gives divine life to the faithful and makes them a community of love in the Holy Spirit.

In his commentary on the Gospel of Saint John, Saint Augustine, the greatest of the Fathers of the Church says: "The first woman called the life and mother of all the living (Gen. 3:20), came forth from the side of Adam asleep" (Gen. 2:21), thus announcing a great joy before the great sorrow of man's fall. The second Adam, Christ, bows his head and sleeps in death; the spouse destined for him came forth from his side while he was asleep.

Explaining Genesis and the creation of woman, St.

Paul writes: "Christ is the head of all creation. . .the Church is his body, He is its head" (Col. I:15,18). In the same way as Adam, Christ slept in His passion, so that the Church, His spouse, could come forth. It is this sleep of death He praises through the mouth of the prophet when He said: "I, when I lie down and sleep I wake again, for the Lord sustains me" (Ps. 3). Pope Saint Leo speaks to us in the same way about Christ and the Church, "His spouse came forth from His flesh with blood and water gushing from His side."

In his *History of France*, Saint Gregory of Tours wrote: "Everyone knows that before the fall, Adam, the first man, prefigured Christ, the Redeemer; Our Lord in His passion let flow blood and water from His open side, and thus gave birth to the virgin Church, without spot, bathed in blood, purified in the sanctifying water, stainless and without blemish."

The same parallel between Adam and Christ, and Eve and the Church exists in the writings of Rufinus of Aquilee when he says: "If you wonder why the blood and water issued from the side of Christ and not from some other part of his body, it is because Eve, the first woman, was formed from the side of Adam, she, the source of sin and death; therefore, the source of redemption and life must flow also from the side of the second Adam."

Let us conclude the many references to the devotion of the Sacred Heart found in the writings of the Fathers of the Church with one last text taken from Saint Bonaventure in the thirteenth century. This text proves that even in the time of Saint Bernard, Saint Francis and Saint Gertrude, not only did the mystics contemplate the Heart of the Savior, but also the entire Church: "So that," he said, "the Church might be formed from the side of Christ on the cross, the word of the Scripture was fulfilled: 'They looked on Him whom they pierced.' A divine decree permitted that one of the soldiers should open the sacred side of Christ in such a way that the price of our salvation was paid with the shedding of the last drop of blood mixed with water flowing from the side of Christ. This blood from the Sacred Heart was to give to the Sacraments of the Church the power to confer grace and become the living waters of eternal life for those who lived in Christ."

*   *   *   *

The theme of the Creation of Eve still used today in

the hymn of the vespers of the Sacred Heart: "From the pierced Heart of Christ, the Church, His spouse was born," can be compared to the image of the open door of Noah's Ark saving the people.   Saint Augustine declares the pierced side of Christ was prefigured by the order given to Noah to open a door in the side of the Ark through which animals were to enter and should not perish in the deluge.

Rupert of Deutz, twelfth century author, also comments on the passage of the Book of Genesis: "This door of the Ark symbolized the wound in the side of Christ, the only opening that allows us to penetrate God Himself." When the spear opened His side, from it gushed water and blood, a profound mystery in which the sins of the world are effaced and we are baptized according to the word of the apostle: 'All of us who have been baptized were baptized in His death.'"

Even before the Redemption, the Church, the mystical spouse of Christ, was symbolized as a bride in the *Canticle of Canticles*. In this Book in which God declared to His spouse: "You have wounded my heart," the commentators took this text and compared it to St. John's account of the piercing of Christ's side with the lance.

Saint Bede, the Venerable, gives this interpretation: "Christ wishing to express His love for the Church, His spouse, became man by assuming human nature." One can apply to Him the following verse of Isaias (53:5): "He was pierced through for our sins." What follows the Canticle verse and the many texts of the New Testament allows us to see why Christ took upon Himself this suffering, "That you might live, O, Universal Church!"

The Fathers of the Church see also in the dove of the *Canticle of Canticles*, another symbol of the love of Christ for His spouse: "Come, my dove, hidden in the clefts of the rock, in the coverts of the cliff" (Cant. cant. 2:14). "The rock was Christ," explains Haymon of Auxerre; "the clefts are the wounds He received, in which the Church, symbolized by the dove, rests, putting its hope in the Passion of Christ."

Thus, in the early Church, devotion to the pierced Heart of Christ flourished. As a matter of fact, the symbolic meaning given to the various verses quoted, the subtle and ingenious way of relating the texts to each other, all this is surpassed by Saint Paul himself when he writes to the Ephesians (5:23-27): "Christ is the Head of the

Church, and saves the whole body. But just as the Church submits to Christ, Christ loves the Church and sacrificed Himself for her, to make her holy. He made her clean by washing her in water with a form of words, so that when Ho took her to Himself she would be glorious, with no speck or wrinkle or anything like that, but holy and faultless."

The apostle gives us this text in the context of his teaching on marriage. "This sacrament reproduces the mystery of love, a mystery of great importance," he said, "of Christ and the Church." This is, then, the ultimate explanation of the Church which He purchased with His own blood (cf. Acts 20:28). From sinful humanity, He made a saintly nation, a royal and priestly race, a chosen people. God had given to Adam a "helpmate like unto himself" (Gen. 2:18). The Church, the new Eve, helpmate and eternal companion of Christ, reflects the Savior himself.

The Church having come forth out of the love of His Heart, Jesus can say of her what Adam said of the first woman: "This, at last, is bone from my bones, and flesh from my flesh" (Gen. 2:23). The Fathers add, "in Christ and the Church is realized the 'they shall be two in one flesh,' a unity symbolized in the water mixed with blood flowing from the open side of Christ on the Cross."

*   *   *   *

The Heart of Christ not only gave birth to the Church, but it still remains the heart of the Church playing its vital role in the mystical Body, just as a human heart functions in a human organism.   From the fullness and generosity of this heart, the Church received and continues to receive its life.   The love of Christ animates it, nourishing it with its tenderness, as it enflamed the heart of the beloved Apostle at the Last Supper: "The Heart of Jesus," explains Geoffrey of Admont (1165), "is the holy scripture itself.   Hidden also in the scriptures is the true spiritual meaning of love which gives interior life to man and makes him live in Christ."

The sacraments, too, nourish the Church.   Baptism infuses in it the life of grace while the Holy Eucharist increases it and allows the Mystical Body to grow. Penance restores grace to the members that have sinned and the Church is again "without speck or wrinkle."   In this way, the spiritual vigor of the Church is maintained and its supernatural strength manifests the life of Christ. She shares with Christ the sentiments of meekness and humility, poverty and chastity, tenderness and kindness. In her are all the treasures of learning and the wisdom of the Holy Spirit of God.

In *The Church*, (4) the Council Fathers spoke thus: "The Holy Spirit was sent on the day of Pentecost in order that He might forever sanctify the Church. . . . He is the Spirit of life, a fountain of water springing up to life eternal. Through him, the Father gives life to men who are dead in sin. . . . The Spirit guides the Church into the fullness of truth, and gives her a unit of fellowship and service. He furnishes and directs her with various gifts both hierarchical and charismatic and adorns her with the fruits of his grace. By the power of the Gospel, He makes the Church grow, perpetually renews her, and leads her to perfect union with her Spouse. The Spirit and the Bride both say to the Lord Jesus, 'Come!' The Heart of Christ maintains the Church in the unity of one Body and one spirit, as in a human body the heart pumps life to all its members." "As all the members of the human body," says the same constitution (7), "though they are many, form one body, so are also the faithful in Christ one body. Also, in the building up of Christ's body there is a flourishing variety of members and functions."

The conciliar text continues: "there is only one Spirit, who according to his own richness and the needs of the ministries, distributes his different gifts for the welfare of the Church (Cor. 12:1-11). The Head of this body is Christ. He is the image of the invisible God and in Him all things came into being. He has priority over everyone and in Him all things hold together. He is the Head of that body which is the Church. All the members ought to be molded into his image until he is formed in them. . . .Made one with his sufferings as the body is one with the head, we endure with him, that with him we may be glorified (Rom. 8:17). From Him, 'the whole body, supplied and built up by the joints and ligaments attains a growth that is of God'" (Col. 2:19).

The growth of the Church manifests itself by the spiritual life that the love of Christ animates in her. This fruition in the Church, a sign of its vigor and growth, is the holiness of each member of the mystical body. For this reason Christ designed His Church. Chapter V of the

Conciliar Constitution brings this idea out in detail. Sinful humanity was compared to a desert. But since the blood and water from the side of Christ flowed to irrigate this arid land, the desert, as it were, flourished in the sanctity of the Church.

Adam of Perseigne, an ancient writer, explains it in a figurative way: "The lance of the soldier opened the side of the Innocent One so that from the blood of innocence mixed with water poured forth a deluge of mercy on the face of the earth. This fountain produced new fruits in abundance." 'Send forth your spirit,' say the Scriptures, 'and all shall be created and you shall renew the face of the earth.'

While on the Cross, Christ gave forth His last breath. The face of the earth renewed, that is, the faith of the Church, brought forth blossoms, roses, lilies of the valley and gardens of perfumes. For in redeeming the world and purifying it from sin, the pouring out of the spotless blood of Christ at the time caused the roses to bud forth in the martyrs, the lilies of the valley in the virgins and created gardens of perfumes in the preachers of the Church. "Let us be, for God," they said, "the good odor of Christ everywhere."

Within the Church, the Holy Spirit produces fruits of grace in the faithful, this holiness draws all those who do not yet know Him to the love of Christ. "All men," declares the Church (13), "are called to belong to the new People of God. This people, while remaining one and unique will be spread throughout the world and will exist in all ages, so that God's will may be fulfilled. In the beginning, God made human nature one. After His children were scattered, He decreed they should at length be unified again."

In this way, the Church simultaneously prays and labors in order that the entire world may become the People of God, the Body of the Lord, and the Temple of the Holy Spirit, and that in Christ, the Head of all, there may be rendered to the Creator and Father of the Universe all honor and glory. Thus the Church seeks to accomplish the ardent call of the Heart of Christ: "Come to me, all of you."

Born out of the Savior's pierced Heart, the Church still lives in Christ, responds to His aspirations and executes His plans of love for humanity. "Jesus Christ and the Church are one," said Jeanne d'Arc. One must then unite this devotion of the Sacred Heart to a very filial and affectionate devotion for the Church. Believing firmly in the love Jesus brought and continues to bring personally to each of us, we shall be better able to see that in Holy Mother Church He gives proof of His love for us. In return, the Church, as the spouse of Christ born from His pierced side, redeemed by the blood of His Son, and animated by His spirit, in a word, the People of God, brings to the Heart of Christ adoration and gratitude. As the dove in the clefts of the rock, we shall hide eternally in His love.

CHAPTER TWO

THE LOVE OF CHRIST
FOR HIS CHURCH

The work of Vatican Council II began with the discussion of the schema on the liturgy. Certain newspaper articles and reviews ridiculed their work with all the facility of the uninformed. Was it really necessary, they said, to bring together more than two thousand Bishops of the Church to discuss details as unimportant as the suppression of certain obsolete rites in the administering of some of the sacraments, or to re-apportion Scripture reading in the Office of the Mass, to give Communion under two species, or even to introduce the use of the vernacular in the liturgy? Singular waste of time for the pastors of souls to care about such trifles, they exclaimed. Others thought Pope John XXIII, in asking the Bishops to discuss this schema first, wanted to allow a certain freedom in the work of the Council.

Such opinions show a deep misunderstanding of the liturgy. They forgot the adage: "The rule of prayer is the rule of faith." The liturgy expresses dogma itself: "The liturgical ceremonies," said Pius XII on September 23, 1956, "are a profession of faith in action. In the liturgy, the Church communicates in abundance the treasures of the 'deposit of faith,' the truths of Christ. Faith and prayer are one. The return to a more simple and authentic way of prayer in the liturgy makes known to the faithful the fundamental aspects of the dogmas of revealed truth."

The pastoral and liturgical functions, far from opposing each other, must intermingle. There cannot be, on the one hand, apostles who preach the word of God, and on the other, mystics devoted entirely to contemplation and the pure praise of God. But the liturgy well understood helps to seek both the glory of God and the salvation of the world. Vatican Council II, in treating the liturgy, did not propose minute details for reforms of the rites, but it set forth the principle of renewal in the Church's worship and prayer.

It also proposed norms for changes based on certain

pastoral considerations. The entire spiritual motivation which was to animate the Council manifested itself in the schema on the liturgy, for example, the importance of the Pascal mystery, the Word of God, and the People of God. On December 4, 1963, Pope Paul VI, in speaking of the Liturgy, could assert: "We shall discover in it a scale of values and obligations to God above all things and prayer as our first duty. God is the primary source of the divine life communicated to us, uniting faith and prayer. The liturgy, hitherto silent, now constitutes an invitation to the world to speak out in joy and true prayer, feel the immense power of life contained in the act of singing together the praises of God and the hopes of men through Christ, Our Savior and in the Holy Spirit."

Indeed, the liturgy permeates the whole Church--the Church in heaven, purgatory, and on earth. The prayer of Jesus Himself ascends to the Father in heaven: "Father," he asks, "glorify your Name!" (Jn. 12:28). Christ is the Master of the liturgy. It is He Himself, living again among His own, revealing the Father to them, bringing the "good news" to the poor, offering for all men His sacrifices and communicating to them, if they will accept it, the

Redemption He merited once and for all on the Cross. These are the mysteries of life on earth lived again, made real. They announce and present again the death and resurrection of Christ.

In the liturgy, the various stages of the life of Christ, both hidden and public, His suffering and glorious life, all are offered to us, that our souls might communicate with it as at the living source Itself. "To possess in us the sentiments of Christ Jesus. . .Crucified with Jesus, we are glorified with Him." Thus, the Church gathered together, as the Apostles around their Master, pray with Him, and even humbly ask Him, as did the disciples: "Lord, teach us how to pray!" The Savior raised His voice and said: "Our Father, hallowed be Thy name, Thy Kingdom come!" and the Church repeats it after Him.

When one understands the Liturgy, one grasps much better how it came forth from the Heart of Christ, how the devotion to the Sacred Heart, born out of the great liturgical act of the Crucifixion, and the mystery of the resurrection, must be accomplished not only with simple practices of private devotion, but in the Eucharistic banquet, in remembrance of the passion of Christ, made present and real among us. Has not Pope Paul VI written: "It is in the Sacred Heart of Jesus that the liturgy finds its origin and beginning. In the sacred Temple of God, the sacrifice of expiation ascends to the Eternal Father. . .It follows, then, that his power to save is utterly certain, since 'he is living forever to intercede for all who come to God through Him'" (Heb. 7:25).

*   *   *

In the Old Testament, God, through Moses, the law-giver, had ordained his own worship: a priesthood had been instituted. Before the building of the temple, they set up in the Hebrew camps the covenant of the Lord, a complete ritual, regulated feasts and ceremonies, oblations, and sacrifices. They knew, also, all the reproaches God addressed to His people: "What are your endless sacrifices to me? The blood of bulls and goats revolts me. Bring me your worthless offerings no more, the smoke of them fills me with disgust. I cannot endure festival and solemnity" (Isaiah I).

Why this disgust of the Most High God? He answered thus: "This people honors me with their lips, but their heart is far from me." After his fall, David expressed himself in the same way: "You take no pleasure in the sacrifice; if I offer a holocaust, you do not partake. My sacrifice is a broken spirit; by a heart bruised and broken, you are not despised." Thus, He cried out: "O God, create in me a pure heart." The true cult of the Sacred Heart is a movement of the heart, true adoration of spirit. On the other hand, external practices emptied of meaning no longer communicate love. They are pharisaical and hypocritical.

The liturgy must not be a collection of words and actions, without meaning, obscure and even hermetical, having lost its real meaning. It must be the collective prayer of the faithful, the People of God, united in one community of charity and expressing together their love of God. For this reason, the Council has simplified, transformed, re-evaluated the liturgy, desiring to make it accessible to the humblest Christian. The Church, the spouse of Christ, could not use gestures and words of formality deprived of meaning for the Christians. The Church must love God with lucidity and sincerity through the heart of all its members. Christians must understand what they are saying to the Lord and say it with love.

But what is the Church without Christ? At the same time, what would liturgy be without the God-Man? "Oh, Father, you did not want any of the ancient holocausts," said the Incarnate Word. "You gave me human form and flesh and I said: 'Behold, I have come to do your will!'"

The true liturgy begins with Christ. He is the temple, the altar, the priest and the victim. The temple is His Body, not made with man's hand, to be destroyed by men and rebuilt in three days, or better still, the temple is His Heart, in which the fullness of God truly resides. In this temple we can find the mercy of God. The Heart of Christ is also the altar of holocaust for the sacrifice of the total gift. It is love alone that can lead the victim to the perfect consummation of itself for the glory of God: "The fire that consumes the holocaust on the altar must not be allowed to go out" (Lev. 6:12-13). The Heart of Christ alone is this ardent furnace of charity capable of fully consuming the victim offered.

Christ is the priest, the unique pontiff of the sacrifice of the New Law, a priest for all eternity according to the order of Melchisedech. At the incarnation, Christ in His humanity was anointed with the oil of divine gladness.

He constitutes the priesthood and alone can offer and immolate Himself. Through Holy Orders, the priest in a special manner participates in the priesthood of Christ. Christians, as members of His mystical body, are the sacred hosts pleasing to God, in the measure of their union with Christ, Who is alone capable of procuring for God the glory He deserves from humanity.

In the temple of God's Heart and on its altar, Jesus offers Himself. From the moment He appeared in this world, even in the womb of the Virgin Mother, He made this oblation of Himself. At the moment of the purification of Mary forty days after His birth, Christ was visibly offered for the first time: "His parents," said Saint Luke, "took Him to Jerusalem to present Him to the Lord." He offered His life on Calvary: "No one takes it from me; I lay it down of my own free will, and as it is in my power to lay it down, so it is in my power to take it up again" (Jn. 10:18). The Father manifests His acceptance of the holocaust of His well-beloved Son in the resurrection on Easter morning, and by letting Him sit at His right side in heaven on the day of His Ascension. The sacrifice is accomplished once and for all, and it is eternally consummated in heaven.

The Apostle Saint John saw it in a vision and described it in the Apocalypse: "Then," he said, "I saw a Lamb that seemed to have been sacrificed. . .and the four animals prostrate themselves before him and with them the twenty-four elders. They were singing a new canticle: 'You are worthy to take the scroll and break the seals of it because you were sacrificed, and with your blood you bought men for God, of every race, language, people and nation. . . .' And I heard the sound of an immense number of angels gathered round the throne and the animals and the elders; there were ten thousand times ten thousand of them and thousands upon thousands shouting, 'The Lamb that was sacrificed is worthy to be given power, riches, wisdom, strength, honor, glory, and blessing'" (5:6-12).

But all the Church is not in heaven. One part of the People of God is on earth. That is why a liturgy parallel to the heavenly liturgy takes place on earth around the sacrificial Lamb. In the Mass, the Church militant sings the glory of the Redeemer. Christ presents again His offering on Calvary to His heavenly Father for the visible

Church. In this way, man's salvation merited on Calvary is secured, the angels in heaven and the elect are filled with joy. The liturgy of Christ, begun in time, offered once and for all on Golgotha, and consummated in eternity came forth from the Heart of Christ in which burns the eternal flame of love.

The Mass of Christ is not an external rite nor a formality. On Calvary, the sacrifice of a bruised and broken heart was offered to God. For what truly counted in the holocaust of the cross was neither the suffering, nor the nails, nor the thirst and anguish, not even death itself. It was Christ's obedience of love: "Father, behold I come to do your will! Be it done! It is consummated!" Jesus Himself told it to us before He left Gethsemani: "Because I love my Father, I do His will." And again: "There is no greater love than to give one's life for those we love."

The liturgy of Christ, then, is the complete recognition of the absolute independence of God, who is Infinite Love. The Eucharist is *par excellence* the act of thanksgiving to a beneficent Father, a prayer of supplication pleading in our favor, the expiation of our sins and failings, "Christ Our Lord, has, indeed, made of the new people a kingdom of priests for God His Father." For in the regeneration of baptism and the unction of the divine Spirit, Christians are anointed to be a spiritual dwelling and a saintly priesthood, offered to God. The love of the Heart of Christ became a liturgy and a sacrifice in the Mass.

Likewise, the heart of the Christian full of love for Our Savior will enable him to transform his life into the liturgy of sacrifice. The liturgy of the Church will be only the official and communal offering of the prayers, actions, and personal sufferings of all Christians. In this way, the celebration of the pascal mystery of Christ continues in the Church. Once again, we state, this mystery has come forth from the love of the Savior and the Heart of Christ contains it all. As Pope Paul VI wrote: "The beginning and the principle of the sacred liturgy is, indeed, the Heart of Jesus, 'the sacred Temple of God.'"

*   *   *

Devotion to the Sacred Heart of Jesus was born in the sacrificial act of Calvary. The true practice of it will lead the Christians through the Eucharist to participate in the death and resurrection of Christ.

Christ was immolated on the cross, or as we said

before, He offered Himself as both priest and victim. The giving up of His last breath was the greatest act in His life and in His entire sacrifice, as Bossuet affirmed. In so doing, Christ's word is fulfilled: "That they may be sanctified, I sacrifice myself." When the soldier pierced Christ's side with his lance, all was ended. His passion revealed the sufferings endured, His patience, charity and mercy. But the love that motivated it was not explicitly manifested. It is His wounded Heart, the symbol of His tenderness, that gives meaning to His passion. Saint John gives witness to his love when he reports what he saw on Calvary and asks us to share his faith.

This beloved apostle, penetrating the interior of the wounded Heart, seized the love of Christ we must all seek after. At this same moment, devotion to the Sacred Heart began with Saint John and Mary, the Mother of Christ, who were present at the Crucifixion, Mary Magdalen and the Holy Women, the saintly people who witnessed the last shedding of His blood mingled with water, touched His mutilated body, and placed the shroud over it.

With His last words: "Father, into your Hands, I commend my spirit," Christ merited for all mankind eternal salvation and offered Himself spotlessly to God. With His own blood, He sprinkled those who were spotted and "purified our consciences from their dead works to render homage to the living God," not with the blood of goats and bulls as under the Old Law. "The death of Christ," to quote Father de Condren, "was the true holocaust consummated by the fire of ardent charity of the victim Himself."

Devotion to the Sacred Heart is essentially the knowledge of this love and affection of Christ and our response to it. In communion with the sacrifice of Christ this devotion is perfected. By keeping in our hearts the love of the Sacred Heart, human and divine, visible and at the same time eternal, devotion to the Heart of Jesus and His love will never cease. It will remain with us in the eternal joys of heaven.

Face to face with this Heart which loved men so much, there can no longer be among the elect the possibility of forgetfulness, ingratitude, and coldness, much less disdain. For the elect and the whole church of heaven, devotion to the Sacred Heart will be consummated. Real devotion to the Sacred Heart must find here on earth participation in the sacrifice of Calvary presented again to our heavenly Father in the Mass. Did not Our Lord say to Saint Margaret Mary: "You will offer me to my Father!" and did He not ask her also to take the Eucharist as often as obedience allowed her?

In one of his apostolic letters Pope Paul VI wrote: "That we may render more honor to the Sacred Heart of Jesus through participation in the most august sacrament, the Eucharist, its most marvelous gift." Our Holy Father adds: "The cult of the Sacred Heart consists essentially in the adoration and reparation of this Heart and is found mainly in the holy mystery of the Eucharist. In the Eucharist, as in other liturgical actions, flows the sanctification of men and the glory of God, the end and aim of all the activities of the Church."

Can the adoration and reparation spoken of by Pope Paul VI be more sincere and more worthy of the Most High than that given Christ at Mass, by the whole Church, the spouse united to Him presenting to Him the pure and sacred Host, the gift that the Father Himself put into the hands of men, that heavenly benediction through which God allows all life to flow, all holiness and all good, the living praise through which all honor and glory ascend to God?

As for reparation, Pius XI in his commentary on the Sacred Heart said: "All the virtue of expiation flows uniquely from the bloody sacrifice of Christ renewed without interruption in an unbloody manner on our altars. In the august sacrifice of the Eucharist, the ministers and the faithful must unite their offerings. The Christian people as one called by the Prince of the Apostles, 'a chosen race, a royal priesthood,' must offer expiatory sacrifices for themselves and for the whole human race."

Devotion to the Heart of Christ must find fulfillment in the Mass and in communion with the Victim who offers Himself for us and for the salvation of the world. The practice of personal or public devotion to the Sacred Heart must lead to the cult and liturgy of the sacrifice of Christ, renewed sacramentally on our altars, or must flow from it. The Holy Hour, for example, is preparation for the Mass. In it, we contemplate the agony of Our Lord in the Garden of Gethsemani, on that historic night of Holy Thursday and Good Friday. The sorrow we have for our sins disposes our soul to unite itself to the actual offering of Christ on the altar. Our devotion to the Sacred Heart makes us participate in this oblation. The Blessed Sacrament, present in our tabernacle or exposed in the monstrance, prolongs our adoration and the offering of the Lamb immolated for us remains as such after the sacrifice of the Mass.

If the devotion to the Sacred Heart is attached to the unique prayer of the Church, or better still, to the prayer of Christ Himself glorifying His Father and interceding for us, it will be preserved from all superstitious practices aimed mainly at sentimental and emotional satisfactions. On the contrary, it will be centered around the sacrifice of Christ, uniting the adoration of the whole world in spirit and in truth, transforming itself in liturgical acts animated by faith, in the expression of an authentic personal or communal devotion. By this very fact alone, it will be virile, vigorous, open and at the same time discreet and radiating. Its fruit will be sanctity. Is not this the same aim ascribed to the devotion of the Heart of Jesus by Pope Pius XII? This devotion will become in the souls of all Christians, according to the expression of Pope Pius XI, "the sum and substance of the faith."

CHAPTER THREE

THE APPEAL OF THE HEART
OF CHRIST TO ALL MEN

When Pope John XXIII convoked the Ecumenical Council, he gave it a double purpose: first, the internal renewal of the Catholic Church that she might be without "speck or wrinkle," as Saint Paul wrote, and secondly, that it serve the cause of Christian unity. Vatican Council II was not a Council for unity as were the former Councils of Lyon or Florence, but by its decisions, decrees, attitudes and projects, all worked together in favor of Christian unity and prepared for it with more or less long-range objectives. For this reason "good Pope John" invited to the Council the Churches separated from Rome by allowing observers to attend the sessions and by creating a Secretariat for Unity similar to the Council.

On November 21, 1964, the final count of 2,137

votes for and eleven votes against the *Decree on Ecumenism* was taken.   Pope Paul VI himself made nineteen last minute changes in that important document so that no text would remain equivocal, vague, or indefinite. Nevertheless, the actions of the Popes, the Council Fathers and especially the decree itself must not be looked upon as acts of opportunism, much less a relaxation of the doctrines of the Church or a compromise with schism and heresy.

On the contrary, these actions and decisions were prompted by the true charity of Christ.   They constitute a protest against the scandal that some Christians take when they look upon a Church divided against itself, and parcelled out.   The Church must be one and unique according to the will of its Divine Founder.   In our day, after centuries of separation, has come the time for pardon of injuries and the removal of anathemas, as was done at the council between the Roman and Orthodox Churches, a time for fraternal meetings, reciprocal marks of interest, respect, and confidence, and a common search for the truth inspired by prayer for strong unity.

All this must be effected in the most sincere loyalty and fidelity to the dogmas of faith, without the spirit of pride or sterile polemics, but with esteem for each other and above all confidence in God. In the opening discourse of the second session of the Council, held on September 29, 1963, Pope Paul VI said and often repeated, "The difficulties to resolve are enormous, the obstacles to overcome almost insurmountable," but recalling the consoling words of Christ, he added: "Things that are impossible for me are possible for God" (Lk. 18:27).

In his apostolic letter, our Holy Father Paul VI indicated again the role to be played by the cult of the Sacred Heart in order to obtain for the Church this unity she is anxiously seeking. He spoke thus: "From the Heart of Christ, the Church received its urgent call to look for every means and all possible support to bring our separated brethren to the perfect unity of the Chair of Peter." These means are pointed out to us in *Ecumenism*. Their study shows they respond fully to the intentions and urgent appeals of the Heart of Christ.

*   *   *

The conciliar decree recalls that the one true Church was instituted by Christ, Our Lord. One of the principal objectives of the Ecumenical Council Vatican II is to promote the restoration of unity among all Christians. The separation of Christians is, indeed, openly opposed to the will of Christ. To re-establish this unity that has been lost, what are the helps, the orientations and the means proposed to all Christians?

We might also ask: What are the Catholic principles of Ecumenism? The first principle is clear in the vision of the will of God to bring all mankind to Christ, the supreme prayer of Christ being, "Father, that they all may be one!" In instituting the loving sacrament of the Eucharist which expresses and makes real the unity of the Church, God sent the Holy Spirit who fills and directs the Church, and unites the faithful intimately in communion with Christ. In Christ and by Christ is the sacred mystery of the unity of the Church. Its supreme model is the trinity of the Persons, the unity of the one true God, Father and Son in the Holy Spirit.

Secondly, the Council asserted that the communities which arose from the separations in the early Church and the serious dissensions that occurred later within it are living by faith in Christ and cannot be accused of the sin of separation. Justified by the faith they received at baptism, and incorporated in Christ, they rightly bear the title of Christians. Besides, the good works that built the Church and give it life can exist outside of the visible limits of the Catholic Church. The written word of God, the life of grace, faith, hope, charity, and other interior gifts of the Holy Spirit, all belong to the whole Christian Church. Yet, we do not hesitate to say: "By the Catholic Church alone, the Church of Christ, can the means of salvation be attained."

Thirdly, the decree states that today by the inspiration of the Holy Spirit, much is accomplished by prayer, word and action to achieve the perfect unity desired by Jesus Christ. All the faithful are exhorted to take an active part in the ecumenical effort. The first effort to make consists in avoiding words, judgments and facts that do not correspond either in justice or truth to the situation of our relationship with them. We should engage in dialogues with them led by well-informed experts, collaborate in all kinds of enterprises, prayer gatherings, and assemblies, all accomplished in prudence and patience.

Catholics should take the first step toward reconciliation, and especially they should look for everything that in the Church must be renewed and brought out so that the image of the Church might reflect sanctity, and the growth of God's Kingdom not be hindered. They should aim also at unity in all that is necessary, but allow freedom to others. Catholics, then, would recognize and appreciate the real Christian values that have their source in the common patrimony and are found also in our separated brethren.

The conciliar decree then treated the practical aspect of ecumenism. It proposed a permanent reform of the Church adhering more faithfully to its true vocation, the renewal of spirit in the heart of Christians, the sincere abnegation of oneself, humility and love of one's work, a fraternal generosity with regard to each other, prayer in common for unity with our separated brethren, mutual reciprocity, teaching of theology and other subject matters, especially the history of the Church, explaining and expounding the doctrine of faith in such a way that would not create an obstacle to dialogue with other Christians, collaborating with them to promote peace and justice, either in developing science and art in a Christian atmosphere, or by bringing relief to those suffering from the miseries of our day: hunger, disasters, ignorance and poverty, housing and the unequal distribution of riches or wealth.

The last part of the conciliar decree is completely devoted to the various churches and communities separated from the Apostolic See of Rome. It brings to light what there is in common between them and the Catholic Church. The conclusion of this study in paragraph twenty-four is a reminder taken from the epistles of Saint Paul to the Romans: "Hope is not deceptive, because the love of God has been poured into our hearts by the Holy Spirit which has been given us" (Rom. 5,5).

*   *   *

Is not this spirit of truth and love that animates the Church and is advocating means for seeking unity symbolized by the water mixed with blood that flowed from the pierced side of Christ? Do not the means proposed by the conciliar documents for a perfect unity of all our separated brethren to the Chair of Saint Peter respond to the urgent call of the Heart of Christ?: "The Charity of Christ presses us." This is really the love of Christ, symbolized by His Heart urging and pressing the

Christians of all confessions to accomplish its priestly prayer: "That all may be one!"

Real ecumenism cannot react juridically on the basis of decrees, but it should be a matter of charity, a movement of the heart of the faithful to follow the example of Christ, their Master. Has not Christ reconciled mankind by shedding His blood? Did He not overthrow all barriers of separation between men, even religious barriers opposing Jews and Gentiles? Does He not wish us to preserve unity in His love by the bonds of peace uniting us? (Eph. 4:3). Why does there not exist in the Christians of today this "one heart" that animated early Christianity, the Heart of the Savior in the interior of the new Church?

What does the Heart of Christ not do for the unity of the Church? Jesus does not ask this unity merely as something reasonable, but rather He wills it in the Word. In fact, never before as in the sacerdotal prayer, has He used so frequently the word "I want". . . .What He wants for His disciples is the very object of His tenderness; it is the Eternal Word speaking to the Father. Here we encounter the triple love of Christ, truly divine yet with human sensibilities and desires drawn forth from His

Heart. "These things I speak in the world in order that they may have my joy made full in themselves" (Jn. 17:13). "Father, I want those you have given me to be with me where I am, so that they may always see the glory you have given me because you loved me. I have made your name known to them. . . so that the love with which you loved me be in them." (*Id.*, 24).

Jesus here speaks as the Son of God; what He wants for those that love Him is the fullness of His presence, the love and joy that our own human tenderness can give to those we cherish. When we speak of the Heart of Christ, we mean not only His sentiments, but the expression of His free will, what He chooses and decides. It is to obtain these joys for those who love Him that Christ prays to His heavenly Father: "That they may be one, as you and I, O Father, are one!"

The sacerdotal prayer of Christ on Holy Thursday revealed His great love for mankind. In it, He gave to His apostles the commandment of unity, not a superficial or moral agreement, but the unity found in the charity expressed in these words to His people: "I am the vine, you are the branches. Abide in me and I in you. Abide in

my love. As I have loved you, love one another." The
Heart of Christ overflows with the charity of love He
wishes to give to all men, for He Himself said: "Risen
from the earth, He will draw all things to Himself."

Here we repeat the words of St. Augustine: "Man
is attracted through the heart." Ah! if all Christians, no
matter to what confession they belong, would know how to
look upon "Him whom they pierced!" If they could
accomplish the wish of Saint John when he tells the account
of the soldier who pierced Christ's side with the lance: "so
that you might also believe. . .that you might believe in
love," could there still exist among them misunderstanding,
hatred, divisions and schisms? Heresy indicates pride of
the intellect. A loving heart does not make a mistake, for
it understands the language of Christ. Schism, on the other
hand, is rivalry in precedence, while love is service, as
Christ, the Son of man gave, who did "not come to be
served but to serve."

Would there still be heresies, if Christians, looking
at the wounds of Christ on the cross, declared with St. Paul
who wished to know and possess only the truth: "The only
knowledge I claimed to have was about Jesus, and only

about Him as the crucified Christ" (Cor. 2:2). Again, would there exist among Christians opposition, schism, rivalry and jealousy, if contemplating Christ on the cross, pierced with a lance for our sins, they cried forth: "As for me, the only thing I can boast about is the cross of Our Lord Jesus Christ" (Gal. 6:14).

May all Christians enter the Heart of Christ into the sheepfold of the Lord where are gathered together those saved from the deluge of sin! May they drink at the source of life, the blood and water flowing from the side of Christ on the cross! May they infuse in their own heart the sentiments and love of the Sacred Heart with all sweetness and humility! Witnessing the stroke of the lance and assisting at the birth of the Church, may they see in it the spouse of Christ, for whom He delivered Himself. They will repeat with Saint Cyprian: "The spouse of Christ cannot be adulterous; she is chaste and spotless. She knows only one house, and respects with modesty the sanctity of only one bed. . .He who abandons the Church of Christ shall not attain the reward of Christ."

Let there not be among Christians the opposition the Jews and the Samaritans have known, the Jews adoring in

Zion and the Samaritans in Garizim. But become true
adorers in spirit and in truth, let them cry out with Saint
Bernard: "It is in this temple, in the sanctuary of your
Heart, O Jesus, before this arch of the covenant, that I
shall adore and praise the name of the Lord "   The
Eucharist, considered a memorial of the passion, and a
testimony of love, this sacrament of the body and blood of
Christ became for all Christians the sign of their unity and
charity. Fed with the same flesh, quenched with the same
blood, they receive one and the same spirit consummated
in unity.

Ludolph of Saxe was correct in writing: "As in the
furnace iron is fused into one piece; thus in the Heart of
Jesus, our love and will become conformed to His love and
will." Shall we, someday, see the union of all Christians
in the one sheepfold of the Good Shepherd?   This
movement will not be accomplished in the immediate
future. To hope for it is not, however, an utopian dream.
Among the various churches, we are already looking for
points of contact, opportunities for coming together, in
faith and love.

Devotion to the Heart of Christ, in so far as it

symbolizes the love it brings to mankind, cannot help but rally all Christians of all origins. How touching it is for us Catholics when we hear and see the devotion our separated brethren have to the Sacred Heart of Christ, we who consider this devotion entirely our own! In the Byzantine liturgy, we are impressed to see the bread cut with a knife soon to become the Body of Christ while the priest utters the words of Saint John: "One of the soldiers, with his lance, opened His side and soon there came out blood and water!"

How we love, too, this invocation in the liturgy of Saint Basil: "O God, you have not forgotten the work of your hands, man, but you have visited your creature in the tenderness of your Heart." How surprising it was for us Catholics to discover in the puritanical Anglican Thomas Goodwin, Cromwell's chaplain, one of the most influential preachers of the Long Parliament, an apostle of the Sacred Heart, half a century before Saint Margaret Mary! His book, *The Heart of Christ in Heaven towards Sinners on Earth*, is a summary of the devotion of the Heart of Christ reminding one of Paray-le-Monial. In it, he describes the Heart of Christ, as it is now in heaven, lovingly and graciously disposed to sinners who come to Him.   He welcomes them, ready to speak with them, expressing His tender pity for all their infirmities, their sins and misery.

In the above examples, we find a common spiritual patrimony with our separated brethren. The sharing of the same goods, the same faith and love brings hope and promise for the future, the unity to come. May the Heart of Christ, our peace and reconciliation, by its triumphant love obliterate all the obstacles which still separate Christians! May this same Heart, king and center of all hearts, gather then all in one Church, born of His Sacred Wound! This People of God, like those in the Acts of the Apostles, will have then only one heart, the Heart of Christ Himself.

CHAPTER FOUR

THE MISSION OF THE CHURCH

The first great revelation made to Saint Margaret Mary in the chapel of the Visitation at Paray-le-Monial took place December 27, 1673. That day, the feast of Saint John the Evangelist, the beloved Apostle to whom Christ told the inexplicable secrets of His Sacred Heart as he leaned on His breast, Christ revealed them also to Saint Margaret Mary: "My Divine Heart is so filled with love for all men. . .that, not being able to contain the flames of its ardent charity, it must spread them through you and manifest itself to others to enrich them with its precious treasures of grace, to pull forth sinners from the abyss of perdition." Thus Our Lord confided the riches of His love to Margaret Mary and made her His apostle that she might transmit to the world the marvels of His Heart.

During His public life, Our Lord said: "Cry out

from the housetops what you have heard in secret!" Every disciple of Christ, after contemplating in the school of His meek and humble Heart, must in turn teach the truth in faith and love. He must share it: "I have seen," said St. John; "my testimony is true and I tell you this that you also may believe!"

One cannot have devotion to the Sacred Heart without being inwardly motivated with the apostolic and missionary spirit of Christ. In the face of so many men who resemble sheep without a pastor, Jesus lamented: "I have pity for the multitude." Again, looking at the immense throng heading for the abyss of perdition, from the gibbet of the cross He saved all men with His blood. Christians, too, and the whole Church animated with deep affection for those not of Christ's fold and for whom Christ also died, must cooperate in the salvation of souls. The Church has always been conscious of her fundamental mission to bring others to Christ.

Frequently, during Vatican Council II as shown in the various decrees, the Church repeated to her members: bishops, priests, religious and laymen alike their duty to bring to others the love of Christ, the Incarnate Word,

Who came to illuminate the world. *The Church* treats in this way the apostolic role of all the People of God, as does *Missions* on the Apostolate of the Laity. As to *Communications* and the declaration on *Christian Education*, their only function is to evangelize the world.

Let us recall the teaching of the Council on the apostolate and the missions. Apostolate and mission are well-nigh synonymous; the objective is identical, but the field of action is different. The devotion to the Sacred Heart is the life-giving source and the powerful motivation of all true apostolates. The words of Pope Paul VI affirm this when he says: "From this Heart, the Church receives its urgent appeals, so that non-Christians also may know with us the only true God and Jesus Christ whom He sent" (Jn. 17:3). The love of the Sacred Heart motivates more than ever the pastoral zeal and missionary spirit of the priests and the faithful to advance the glory of God. With eyes fixed on the eternal love Christ gave witness to, they will concentrate their efforts on one aim: to communicate to all men the infinite treasures of Christ.

*   *   *

The documents of Vatican Council II strengthen the

mission of the Church and affirm its functions. In founding the Church, Christ wished to bring to all men the salvation He merited for them by dying on the cross. "The Church received the commandment of Christ to teach all nations until the end of time. Therefore, she accepts the words of the Apostle: 'I should be punished, if I do not preach the Gospel!' (I Cor. 9:16). Indefatigably, it continues to send forth heralds of 'Good News' until the new missions are fully able to take upon themselves the work of salvation. The Holy Spirit guides it to cooperate in the total realization of God's design who made Christ the principle of salvation. The Church unites prayer and work to make the whole world the People of God, the Mystical Body of Christ and the Temple of the Holy Spirit" . . . (*The Church*, 17).

In virtue of its innate qualities of universality and obedience to the commandment of Christ (Mk. 16:16), the Church puts forth all its effort to proclaim the 'Good News' to all creation. . .Commissioned by the Lord Christ to bring salvation to every man, it is consequently bound to proclaim the Gospel. *Communications* (3) reiterates this mission when it says: "For this the Church was founded: that by spreading the kingdom of Christ everywhere for the glory of God the Father, she might bring all men to share in Christ's saving redemption; and that through them the whole world might in actual fact be brought into relationship with Him."

All activity of the Mystical Body directed to the attainment of this goal is called the apostolate and the Church carries it on in various ways through all her members. By its very nature the Christian vocation is also a vocation to the apostolate. No part of the structure of a living body is merely passive, but each has a share in the functions as well as in the life of the body. So too, in the Body of Christ, which is the Church, the whole body "according to the functioning in due measure of each single part derives its increase" (Eph. 4:16).

But the mission of the Church to bring salvation to all souls involves more than this purely spiritual and eternal aspect. Men possess a body also, live in society and have a temporal existence. Grace acts on nature; the divine spirit teaches the human mind; purely worldly activities are influenced and sublimated by the Gospel. In *Laity* (5), we read: "The work of the Redemption of Christ which concerns essentially the salvation of men involves also the renewal of the whole temporal order. Hence, the mission of the Church is not only to bring to men the message of Christ and His grace, but also to penetrate and perfect the temporal order with the spirit of the Gospel. Though the spiritual and temporal order are distinct, they are united in the one plan of God. God Himself wishes in Christ to regain the whole world. . . ."

Who shall do this work of evangelization so much desired by Christ and the Church? Who shall go to take Christ to all nations and live with them? The Council answers: "As members of the living Christ, all the faithful have been incorporated into Him and made like unto Him through baptism, confirmation, and the Eucharist. Hence, all are duty-bound to cooperate in the expansion and growth of His Body, so that they can bring it to fullness as swiftly as possible" (*Missions*, 36).

To be sure, responsible people are needed for this work of the apostolate, organizers, those who will give themselves to the people. This is the first duty of the Bishops, as stated in *Missions* (6): "This duty must be fulfilled by the order of bishops, whose head is Peter's successor, and with the prayer and the cooperation of the whole Church. . . ."

As members of the body of Bishops which succeeds the college of Apostles, all Bishops are consecrated not just for some one diocese, but for the salvation of the entire world. Christ's mandate to preach the gospel to every creature (Mk. 16:15) primarily and immediately concerns them, with Peter and under Peter (*Missions*, 38).

The decree on the pastoral duties of the Bishops recommends that they concern themselves with those parts of the world where the word of God has not yet been made known. After the Bishops, the entire Church, the People of God must go and proclaim the 'Good News' of Christ. The priests must cooperate with the Bishops. By means of their very ministry, which deals principally with the Eucharist as the source of perfecting the Church, they are in communion with Christ the Head and are leading others to this communion. Hence, they cannot help realizing how much is yet wanting to the fullness of that Body, and how much, therefore, must be done, if it is to grow from day to day (*Missions*, 39).

The priests shall call to mind that they must have at

heart the care of all the Churches.   Hence, priests belonging to dioceses which are rich in vocations should show themselves willing and ready with the permission or at the urging of their own bishop, to exercise their ministry in other regions, missions, or activities which suffer from a shortage of clergy (*Priests*, 10).   The consecrated souls in contemplative communities by their prayers, works of penance and sufferings have a very great importance in the conversion of souls since it is God who sends workers into the fields, opens the minds of non-Christians to hear the Gospel and make fruitful in their hearts the word of salvation (*Missions, 40).*

Vatican Council II consecrated an entire decree to the apostolate of the laity, the whole People of God.   They comprise the Church.   After them are the pastors.   Though the Popes have reminded them frequently in the past forty years, never has their role in the evangelizing of the world been so specifically made known and precisely and clearly explained as by the conciliar documents.   "The mission of the Church," says *Laity* (6), "concerns the salvation of men which is to be achieved by faith in Christ and by His grace.   Hence, the apostolate of the Church and of all her members is primarily designed to manifest to the world Christ's message by words and deeds and to communicate His grace to the world. That work is done mainly through the ministry of the word and of the sacraments, which are entrusted in a special way to the clergy. But the laity too have their very important roles to play if they are to be 'fellow-workers for the truth'" (Jn. 3:18).

Missions (41) declares: "Laymen cooperate in the Church's work of evangelization. As witnesses and at the same time as living instruments they share in her saving mission." Baptism by its very nature makes of all the faithful the People of God and a priestly race, bound by this very fact to the apostolate: "The laity," the Council specifies, "derive the right and duty with respect to the apostolate from their union with Christ their head" (*Laity*, 3). They exercise a genuine apostolate by their activity on behalf of bringing the gospel and holiness to man, and on behalf of penetrating and perfecting the temporal sphere of things through the spirit of the gospel (*Laity*, 2). In this way, they are called by God to exercise their apostolate in the world as a kind of leaven and with the vigor of the spirit of Christ.

There are many persons, the Council tells us, who can hear the Gospel and recognize Christ only through the laity who live near them (*Laity*, 13).

*   *   *

In the above paragraphs, we have seen the apostolic and missionary tasks of the Church clearly defined. Each and every Christian must share in them according to his state of life and function belonging to the People of God. But how will this apostolate be accomplished? The first apostolic activity and the most fundamental required of all those who work in evangelizing mankind is the life of grace and union with Christ. *Laity* (4) states: "Since Christ in His mission from the Father is the fountain and source of the whole apostolate of the Church, the success of the lay apostolate depends upon the laity's living union with Christ. For the Lord has said: 'He who abides in me, and I in Him, he bears much fruit; for without me you can do nothing'" (Jn. 15:5).

The same decree (3) declares: "The apostolate is carried on through the faith, hope and charity which the Holy Spirit diffuses in the hearts of all the members of the Church." Let each one remember that he can have an impact on all men and contribute to the salvation of the whole world by public worship and prayer as well as by penance and voluntary acceptance of the labors and hardships of life. By such means does the Christian grow in likeness to the suffering Christ (16).

In *Missions* (36), we read: "Let all realize that their first and most important obligation toward the spread of the faith is this: to lead a profoundly Christian life. For their fervor in the service of God and their charity toward others will cause new spiritual inspiration to sweep over the whole Church."

The second way to practice the apostolate is by giving witness, the personal witness of the apostles in the Christian life. This idea is expressed in *Laity* (6) thus: "The very testimony of their Christian life and good works done in a supernatural spirit, have the power to draw men to belief in God."

By this witness of charity, the members of the Church will be united in Christ. Christians are called to engage in the apostolate as individuals or in groups. Hence the group apostolate of Christian believers happily corresponds to a human and Christian need and at the same time signifies the communion and unity of the Church in Christ, who said: "Where two or three are gathered together in my name, there am I in the midst of them: (Mt. 18:20).

Finally, the witness of the charity of Christ through His disciples will benefit all mankind. *Laity* (8) declares: "Some works by their very nature can become especially vivid expressions of this charity. Christ the Lord wanted these works to be signs of His messianic mission. The Church claims works of charity as her own inalienable duty and right."

The Christian witness, however would not be complete without making known Christ and our salvation through Him. "Faith comes from hearing." How can one believe in Jesus Christ, if He is not preached? *Laity* (6) adds, "a true apostle looks for opportunities to announce Christ by words addressed either to non-believers with a view to leading them to faith, or to believers with a view of instructing and strengthening them, and motivating them toward a more fervent life."

The decree on the *Missions* (6) is still more explicit when it says, "The specific purpose of this missionary activity is evangelization and the planting of the Church among those peoples and groups where she has not yet taken root. . . .The chief means of this implantation is the preaching of the Gospel of Jesus Christ. The Lord sent forth His disciples into the whole world to preach this Gospel. Thus reborn by the Word of God (Pt. 1:23) men may through baptism be joined to that Church which, as the Body of the Incarnate Word, is nourished and lives by the Word of God and by the Eucharistic Bread (Acts 2:43).

To preach the Gospel to all creatures, the Church and its apostles use all the appropriate means. Urged by the obligation to bring salvation to every man, the Church judges it part of her duty to preach the news of redemption with the aid of the instruments of social communication and to instruct mankind as well in the worthy use of these means.

Precisely for this reason, the Church concerns itself with schools and education. To fulfill the mission Christ confided to her to proclaim the mystery of salvation to all men and to restore all things in Christ, Holy Mother the Church must be concerned with the whole of man's life, even the earthly part of it insofar as that has a bearing on his heavenly calling. She has, therefore, a role to play in the progress and spread of education. The Catholic school prepares the students to serve the advancement of the Kingdom of God on earth.

The conciliar decrees remind us of what is and what should be the apostolic and missionary activity of the Church, "nothing else and nothing less than a manifestation or epiphany of God's will and the fulfillment of that will in the world and in world history. In the course of this history, God plainly works out the history of salvation by means of mission" (*Missions*, 9).

To be sure, those men who have not heard the message of salvation will not be lost, if they remain faithful to their conscience, provided they have not falsified it or stifled it. This does not mean, however, that their salvation will be easier. More than ever, the Church must proclaim, therefore, to all creatures the Word of God.

"Though God," says *Missions* (7), "in ways known to Himself can lead those inculpably ignorant of the Gospel to that faith without which it is impossible to please Him, yet a necessity lies upon the Church, and at the same time a sacred duty, to preach the Gospel. Hence missionary activity today as always retains its power and necessity."

* * *

Here we might ask: What benefits does the apostle, whoever he is, in whatever manner and place he proclaims the Gospel draw from devotion to the heart of Christ? Is not the mission the Church gives him with its responsibilities and the fire of his zeal sufficient? If it were a question of a totally human propaganda, requiring only courage and a certain technique, we could answer, "Yes." Evangelizing the world is the work of grace. If the Church's mission is to make known the message of salvation, it is because she is the spouse of Christ, born out of the wound in His side.

It is not the apostles who convert, but Christ alone; His love was the only force that could overcome Paul on the road to Damascus, tear Saint Augustine completely away from sin, totally change the mode of life of Charles de Foucauld! God chooses the weak to overcome the strong, the ignorant to confound the learned and wise in the ways of the world! Christ warns the Apostles not to become proud in their success. "When you have done all you have been told to do, say, we are merely servants. We have done no more than our duty" (Lk. 17:10).

Christ is the unique Apostle and missionary. During His earthly life and throughout the Church today, He continues to proclaim the "Good News" until the end of the world. Because He loves men passionately, as He said at Paray-le-Monial, He wants to save them from perdition, seek and find those who have strayed away. The cult of the Sacred Heart, then, is to stir love in the heart of the apostles and motivate them to lead souls to Christ.

The soul truly devoted to the Sacred Heart in the school of this Heart, meek and humble, can only desire the salvation of souls and give himself ardently to the apostolate. This zeal for souls did not come forth from a purely human feeling of pity for those unfortunate enough not to be born in the faith. Nor did it spring from a need to give oneself naturally to activity. The apostolate is a response of faith to the love of Christ. Pope Paul VI asked the apostles to fix their eyes on the example of the eternal love Christ came to manifest.

Thus, the apostolate must take its source in love of the Savior. How has this love manifested itself? Saint Paul answers us: "We were still helpless when at his appointed moment Christ dies for sinful men. It is not easy to die even for a good man. . .but what proves that God loves us is that Christ died for us while we were still sinners" (Rom. 5:6-8).

In his Epistle to the Ephesians (2:4-6), the Apostle speaks in the same way: "God loved us with so much love that he was generous with his mercy: When we were dead through our sins, he brought us to life with Christ--it is through grace that you have been saved; he raised us up with him and gave us a place with Him in heaven, in Christ Jesus." Did not Christ Himself say: "The Good Shepherd gives his life for his sheep?" "My Father loves me because I offer my life" (Jn. 10:11 & 17). "There is no greater love than to lay down one's life for those he loves."

If we believe God loves us in this way, if we meditate without ceasing the numerous and continuous proofs of His love, if our souls were full of gratitude for the Heart of the Savior who showed us such great love, how can we refrain from wanting to resemble Christ and imitate Him? The Christian must imitate in spirit the words and actions of His Master. Since Christ loved the impious, the sinner, and those not of His sheepfold, we too must love them who know not Christ or the Gospel. Thus, our hearts shall become like Christ's.

Jesus not only offers His Heart to us as a model, but from it come the urgent appeals sent forth by Our Holy Father, Pope Paul VI to make known to all non-Christians the only true God and Him whom He has sent, Jesus Christ. "The Charity of Christ urges," said the Apostle and pressed by this love, Saint Paul adds: "This is the Christ we proclaim, this is the wisdom in which we thoroughly train every one and instruct everyone to make them perfect in Christ. It is for this I struggle wearily on" (Col. 1:28-29). "The heart of Paul," says Saint Chrysostom, "was the Heart of Christ."

What appeal does the heart of Christ make, we might ask? "Come to me, all of you!" and again, "If anyone thirst let him come to me and drink." Father, glorify your Son. . .that He may give life eternal to those you have given Him, and life everlasting that they may know you, the only true God, and Him whom you sent, Jesus Christ. The appeals of the Heart of the Savior, silent and interior but urgent come especially from the true love of the Cross to all souls. "When I shall have been raised above the earth, I shall draw all things to myself!"

Nevertheless, so that Christ might bring the "Good News" today to the poor, deliver the captives, give sight to the blind, He needs heralds and messengers who will answer His appeals: "Come follow me, I shall make you fishers of men," and "Raise your eyes and see the fields are ripe for the harvest." "Go to the ends of the world." These requests of the Heart of Christ to save all men inflame the hearts of His disciples with zeal in their vocation to the Apostolate, provide them with the generosity to respond, the courage and heroism to undertake their missionary tasks and persevere in their fulfillment in spite of difficulties and failures.

The Heart of Christ, furnace of charity, has embraced the hearts of all men. In turn, these hearts will inflame the hearts of other men, and from one to the other, heart to heart, the fire of love which the savior came to kindle on earth will conquer the world even to its remotest extremities.

Devotion to the Heart of Jesus will not only fill with love those who in heaven will form the "Choir of the

Apostles," but it will provide them with ways of carrying on their missionary endeavors, a work more frequently painful than elating. In fact, the task to be accomplished, however noble it might be, is not a human one of education and civilization. Naturally speaking, the individual would benefit personally and socially in his work of evangelization. But the objective to be attained is more than that. Our Holy Father Paul VI reminds us of it when he says: "Communicate to all men the infinite treasures of Christ."

Therefore, it is not a question of favoring or promoting one race or civilization, their customs, social classes, economy and politics, but rather the only aim is to proclaim Christ and Him crucified, to preach penance for the salvation of souls, to lead them to the faith of Christ, the Redeemer. In a word, it is to inculcate in the hearts of men the divine life of Christ more abundantly, that He might animate souls more and more with His love.

In this apostolate of love supernatural by its very nature, modeled on the meek and humble heart of Christ, the apostle will not come to be served, but to serve. He will show simplicity and patience, and as the apostle St.

Paul states he "will be clothed in sincere compassion, in kindness and gentleness. Bear with one another. Forgive each other. . .put on love. And may the peace of Christ reign in your hearts" (Col. 3:12-14).

In accomplishing his work, the apostle of the Heart of Christ will seek only the glory of God. Failures will not discourage him, overwhelm or dishearten him, for he knows God succeeds in spite of the failures of His apostles and that he must participate in the passion of Christ. What he accomplishes, he will do in obedience to the Church, in filial docility to this prudent and courageous holy Mother. If necessary, he will go so far as to give his life-blood to bear witness to Christ, His Redeemer.

The true apostle wishes to love Christ in return, as Christ loved His apostles and the souls He evangelized. Like the first Apostles, all of whom became martyrs, he will give witness to Christ even with death as the following account reveals.

In the year 177 of our era, in the reign of the Emperor Marcus-Aurelius, a terrible persecution broke out in Gaul and raged particularly in the city of Lyon. Among the martyrs, there was a deacon from Vienna, named

Sanctus. The following year, the Christians of Lyon, writing to their brethren in Asia and Phrygia, told the story of his martyrdom thus: "Sanctus endured with superhuman courage all the horrible treatments of men. To all the questions asked him, he was happy to answer: 'I am a Christian!' The governor and the persecutor rivaled cruelty against him. When they had no other torments to inflict on him, they decided to apply burning copper blades on the most delicate parts of his body. These parts were burned; but without flinching he remained firm and steadfast, as if refreshed and fortified by the celestial source of living water that flowed from the side of Christ."

This story tells the beginning of the whole apostolate, the missionary life, and the heroism of the servant of Christ, the perfect witness to proclaim to the world that Christ is the Son of God and the savior of men. It testifies how even at that time long before the cloistered mystics of the middle ages, the martyrs in the arenas and amphitheaters drew from the Sacred Heart of Christ a superhuman energy to return Him love in the face of a pagan world, and spread His Kingdom in this world.

According to the great Dominican preacher

Lacordaire, in each succeeding generation Christ raises up apostles and martyrs to follow Him and He finds them willing to take up the cross. As the deacon Sanctus, so may all who spread the Kingdom of God on earth by the testimony of their suffering and bloodshed be refreshed and fortified by the love of the Sacred Heart of Jesus and by the celestial source of living water that flowed from the side of Christ!

CHAPTER FIVE

THE RESPONSE OF THE
PEOPLE OF GOD

In his presentation of the French edition of the decree on
the *Adaptation and Renewal of the Religious Life*, his
excellency, Bishop LeBourgeois, then Superior General of
the Eudist Fathers, wrote:

"The importance given by the Council to the
theology of the episcopate, the study of the apostolate
under the direction of the Bishops and the promotion of the
laity, seems to present a problem to many of the faithful.
Is the religious life as we know it fulfilling a need in the
Church? The criticisms raised today against this type of
living, from easy pleasantries about religious habits and the
number of women's congregations, to attacks against the
vows of religion considered impossible burdens for human
nature to carry, against contemplative orders accused of

abandoning the world and neglecting the apostolate at a time when the need for evangelization is imperative, and against active orders which, they say, should leave their present work to undertake the tasks of Catholic action with tho laity, are numerous."

The Council did not understand religious life in this way. In *The Church*, chapter V treated the universal call of all Christians to sanctity, then consecrated chapter VI, a sort of corollary to it, to the religious state in the Church and the value of religious consecration. The decree on the *Religious Life* voted on October 11, 1965, explains and clarifies this chapter.

The conciliar Fathers actively concerned themselves with it, and expressed it by an overwhelming vote when the schema was presented to them, for the renewal of the spirit in religious institutes and their adaptation to the needs of the Church today. "The two words, renewal and adaptation, are inseparable," writes Bishop LeBourgeois. This does not mean religious institutes are outmoded, but it shows the willingness to better respond to the needs of the Church today by returning to their origin for inspiration.

The practical application of the principles of renovation and adaptation in the religious life is to be determined by the institutes themselves. We are not concerned with this matter here. What does interest us is the conciliar decree on the Church. Chapter six of this decree gives the precise explanation of the nature and aims of religious life. As Bishop LeBourgeois stressed, "One can affirm that no Council before Vatican II ever sketched a more beautiful image of the religious life, indicated more clearly its place in the Church, outlined in a better way for the congregations themselves, in the spirit of self-esteem and moderation, the rules to follow in order to remain faithful to one's vocation."

Can we not say that religious life in effect is a state of consecration and devotion to the Sacred Heart, a gift of oneself to the love of Christ? Does not the devotion to the Sacred Heart that the faithful in the world practice also fulfill this religious consecration? Indeed, the source is the same, the purpose identical, and the benefits flowing from it similar, whether it is a question of the cult of the Sacred Heart or the religious life. The religious life, however, a total dedication of oneself to Christ and His Church, receives from devotion to the Sacred Heart, a spiritual depth and intensity of love which cannot be forfeited.

*   *   *

When his twenty-year-old daughter asked permission to enter the convent, Montalembert, the eighteenth century French author, who was at that time writing *The Monks of the West*, explained: "Who is this Invisible Lover Who died on the gibbet eighteen hundred years ago, and can still attract to Himself youth, beauty, and love? Who appears with such glamour souls cannot resist, seizes them and makes them His own, transforming them flesh and blood into Himself? What is this Lover? Contrary to any romantic ideas, one does not enter the convent disappointed in love, one finds hope, security, and happiness, "Him Whom she loves," the God-man, a Real Person, a living Being to whom she attaches herself with her every fiber forever.

Devotion to the Sacred Heart is the discovery that Jesus loves us. And we have believed in Love! "He loved me and delivered Himself for me." Religious consecration has the same origin. As Rene Bazin once wrote: "One does not sacrifice beauty, joy, and life for something imaginary; nor shut himself or herself up in a monastery or convent, or live chaste and poor, without any desire but obedience, for forty years, because one likes white artificial flowers and silence, or the smell of burning incense. There is something else." More precisely, we should say there is "Someone else," for a thing would not be enough, not even the most beautiful dreams, the most sublime thoughts, the highest ideal of generosity, or the most genial philosophy.

A man or a woman does not sacrifice riches and desires, resources and passions for a myth, an idea, or even a moral. Their heart does not give itself to another heart it imagines or creates for himself as the most beautiful and best of all hearts. This is a frequent illusion and often tragic, for appearances are deceiving, and dreams disillusioning. From enchanted hopes follow sad realities. Let us not accuse man of having only a human heart, capable of many promises, but weak, changeable, and deceptive.

United to the Heart of the God-Man, the human heart is assured of a constant, total, and powerful love. This heart is the receptacle of divine charity, eternal and infinite as God Himself Who said: "With an eternal love, I have loved you!" The Heart of Christ, human and sensitive as our own, has also experienced emotions, and can embrace us with all tenderness. His will directs and dominates His decisions. Not subject to instinct, He is strong, virile, and exacting, for true love is not softness or languid affection, but the giving of oneself even in excess.

In the discovery of this three-fold love of the Heart of Christ came forth devotion to the Sacred Heart and the religious vocation. Both are a response to the loving charity of Christ in the dedication of oneself to His Sacred Heart. It is the offering of all our works and actions, our whole being to Him, pains and sufferings, as Saint Margaret Mary put it, not only our prayers and participation in the sacraments and the apostolate, but also our entire human existence, public and private, social life, work life, married and family life, and our relationship with all. This gift of oneself is not limited to a single act of passing generosity, but constitutes a conscious dedication of one's whole being to the Heart of Christ, inspired by His love.

By baptism, we are purified and sanctified, and

made to enter into the Kingdom of God, uniting us to Christ for God's glory, transforming us into His sons of adoption. For by baptism, the love of God takes root in our heart through the Holy Spirit. In delivering himself freely to the Heart and love of Christ, the Christian ratified the offering of himself to God and by this act of faith became a divine possession, abandoning himself to divine love never to be retracted.

Religious consecration, however, goes even further. Dedication to the love of Christ symbolized by the Sacred Heart not only rejects selfishness and sin, but accepts all else in return for the love of Christ. It is exclusive and does not accommodate itself to anything that is not uniquely love. By their vows or other sacred engagements embraced in the vows, he who consecrates himself to God gives himself entirely to God, to be loved by all men and ordained in the service of the Lord for His honor with a new and special title.

By baptism, he was already dead to sin and consecrated to God. By his profession of the evangelical counsels made to the Church, he wishes to gather in greater abundance the fruits of his baptismal grace and to liberate himself from any burden that could hinder him in his practice of perfect charity or prevent him from consecrating himself more intimately to God's services. This consecration is all the more perfect by its close and stable ties that better reproduce the image of Christ united to the Church, its spouse, by an indissoluble bond (*The Church*, 44).

The decree on the *Religious Life* (5) expresses itself in the same way when it says: "The members of each community should recall above everything else that by their profession of the evangelical counsels they have given answer to a divine call to live for God alone not only by dying to sin (Rom. 6:11), but also by renouncing the world. They have handed over their entire lives to God's service in an act of special consecration which is deeply rooted in their baptismal consecration and which provides an ampler manifestation of it."

Thus chosen by Christ, for as He said to His elect: "You have not chosen Me, but I have chosen You," called to total dedication, the soul committed to religious life is able to repeat the Canticle verse: "I have found Him whom my Heart loves. I have seized Him and I shall not let Him go." Through religious consecration, the soul wishes to live for God alone. In Christ Jesus, she has discovered and encountered the God-Man made manifest by divine revelation. She takes the Savior for her unique spouse, the sovereign king on whom she depends for love. Thus, the promises of baptism are lived to perfection. In this way, devotion to the Heart of Christ attains its highest degree.

By this consecration to the Sacred Heart, the religious state will truly become an abode of the human being in Christ, the Beloved. "The will to belong to Christ and Him alone becomes irrevocable," says Saint Margaret Mary. Once the vows are pronounced, this consecration to the Sacred Heart helps one to remain faithful to Christ and grow in His love.

*   *   *

In order to arrive at perfect union with Christ, and to respond completely to His infinite love, several conditions are indispensable: contemplation, sacrifice, and the imitation of Christ. How do these compare with devotion to the Sacred Heart? Contemplation. Did not Saint John repeat after the prophet Zacharius: "They looked on Him whom they pierced." Sacrifice. Saint Paul counsels us: "In your minds you must be the same as Christ Jesus. His state was divine, yet he did not cling to his equality with God, but emptied himself to assume the condition of a slave!" (Phil. 2:6-7). Imitation. Christ Himself invites us to imitate Him "Come to me and learn of me, for I am meek and humble of heart," He says.

In the various religious states including the active life, priority is given to prayer and contemplation. Love demands that we look continuously on the Beloved. Could one imitate Christ in his life, if he did not first contemplate the mind and heart of Christ? In substance, *Religious Life* (6), states that they who profess the evangelical counsels seek God first and love Him above all, He who has first loved us that they may in every circumstance live hidden in God with Christ. The religious cultivates with constant care the spirit of prayer, prayer taken from the true sources of Christian spirituality. The Sacred Scripture is in their hands every day for reading and meditation, so they may learn Jesus Christ.

Prayer, moreover, is not an intellectual exercise, a sequence of ideas, a game of rationalization. On the contrary, it is the loving attention given to Christ with the eye of faith and a heart burning with love for Him. Charmed by the beloved, the heart of the religious disposes itself entirely to the love Christ gives in return. We can well understand, then, the transports of the mystics. They sought the love of Christ, and Christ in return gave them the grace to understand it and experience it.

Saint Margaret Mary, for example, saw the Heart of Christ enthroned in flames, more ravishing than the sun, transparent as crystal, crowned with thorns and a cross over it, the loving wound in its side. Through this heart, she experienced ardent charity. God granted her desire and rewarded her love. This case is not exceptional. Only with the eyes of faith will the contemplative soul be guided in the darkness of this world. By prayer and joy in the tenderness of Christ will she be sustained and persevere in infinite charity: "He who loves me," says our Lord, "I shall love him and manifest Myself to him" (Jn. 25:21).

To achieve complete union with God and possess Him fully, one must, indeed, sacrifice oneself. When one is engrossed in material possessions that bring us pleasure and satisfaction, one cannot see God, hence the need for religious vows. It is a mistake to consider them an impoverishment, deprivation, frustration, or limitation either of our natural tendencies and needs or of our personality. Does not all authentic love restrain the heart to the object to be loved? Love intensifies and becomes all-embracing. When interests are numerous, love becomes lukewarm, solicited by too many appeals. Give man, rather, an exceptional person to love, and he will become exceptional. Propose to him, above all, the only perfect human heart to whom divinity itself is united, then what ardor will not consume him?

Before a poor human heart can change in the furnace of love of the Sacred Heart, it must be despoiled of all its impurities. To take the example proposed by Saint John of the Cross, the divine flame of charity can glow only when the darkness which obscures our faith and hinders us from being perfectly identified with Christ's love is removed. The moisture in the wood pile must first be dried out before the fire can begin to burn. Thus, the heart of man cannot be transformed into the Heart of Christ, until it rejects completely what in it is repugnant to Christ or does not conform to His will.

The Church (44) makes clear the need for practicing

the evangelical counsels founded on the word and example of Christ. *Religious Life* also makes known the exclusive role of the religious embraced in the vows: poverty, chastity, and obedience. "That chastity which is practiced 'on behalf of the heavenly Kingdom' (Mt. 19:12), and which religious profess deserves to be esteemed as a surpassing gift of grace. For it liberates the human heart in an unique way (I Cor. 7:32-35) and causes it to burn with greater love for God and all mankind" (12).

The same decree (13) states: "Poverty voluntarily embraced in imitation of Christ provides a witness which is highly esteemed, especially today. . . .By it, a man shares in the poverty of Christ, who became poor for our sake when before He had been rich, that we might be enriched by His poverty" (II Cor. 8:9; Mt. 8:20).

It continues: "Through the profession of obedience, religious offer to God a total dedication of their own wills as a sacrifice of themselves; they thereby unite themselves with greater steadiness and security to the saving will of God" (14).

By its very nature, love demands detachment from pleasure, earthly treasures and domineering pride. Love

demands love in return.   Whether it is a question of
devotion to the Sacred Heart or dedication to the love of
Christ in the religious state, self-sacrifice is necessary for
a total consecration of oneself.   Saint Margaret Mary, a
contemplative and confidante of the Sacred Heart could
write: "You will be pleasing to the Heart of Christ when
you abandon yourself to Him in such a way that He will be
your faculty of hearing, the look in your eyes, the light of
your understanding, the affections of your will, the love in
your heart, with no reservations but the desire to please
and love Him above all things."

Thus, we see the practice of the vows is not a
negative mortification, but a love reaching out in imitation
of Christ and united to Him.   Poverty, chastity, and
obedience are not objectives in themselves.   One seeks
them only to put on Christ.   He was poor, humble,
obedient and chaste, declaring "Who sees me, sees my
Father"; in like manner, a human being, religious man or
woman devoted to the Heart of Christ by the invasion of
His love is transformed by it. Jesus communicates Himself
so completely to these souls that they appear other Christs
rather than purely human beings. *The Church* (46) puts it:

"The evangelical counsels voluntarily undertaken according to each one's personal vocation, contribute greatly to purification of heart and spiritual liberty. They continually kindle the fervor of charity. As the example of so many saintly founders show, the counsels are especially able to pattern the Christian man after that manner of virginal and humble life which Christ the Lord elected for Himself, and which His Virgin Mary also chose."

Devotion to the Sacred Heart and the vows of religion sanctify the human heart. As the Gospel says: "By their fruits you shall know them." This sanctity is characterized by a three-fold manifestation: adoration, reparation, and apostolic zeal. "This kind of worship," said Pius XII, "allows man to better honor and love God. By rendering homage to the Sacred Heart of the Redeemer, the faithful satisfy their obligation of serving God and obey His divine commandment: 'You shall love the Lord your God with your whole heart, with your whole soul, with your whole mind and with all your strength.'"

Likewise, the Heart of Jesus, bruised by our offenses and sins, demands reparation. The soul devoted to the Sacred Heart shares in the role of the redeeming

Christ and by his love repairs the wound inflicted on His Sacred Heart. Finally, devotion to the Sacred Heart includes the apostolate: "Love one another as I have loved you." It provides the source and help necessary to carry through the command of God. In 1965, His Eminence Monsignor Le Brun wrote: "How could he be the militant Christian the Church desires, the Christian filled with zeal and devotion to the service of his brethren, if these motives do not proceed from Christ's love?"

The conciliar documents we have quoted on religious life also enumerate the fruits issued from the Heart of Christ. As indicated in *The Church* (44): "The religious state reveals in a unique way that the kingdom of God and its overmastering necessities are superior to all earthly considerations. Finally, to all men it shows wonderfully at work within the Church the surpassing greatness of the force of Christ the King and the boundless power of the Holy Spirit."

Religious Life (6) makes other declarations stating that those who profess the evangelical counsels love and seek God before all else, that the members of those communities which are totally dedicated to contemplation give themselves to God alone in solitude and silence and through constant prayer and ready penance. "The main task of monks is to render a service at once simple and noble within the monastic confines to the Divine Majesty" (*Id.*, 9).

Reparation is part of this service to the divine Majesty, and one of the purposes of the Holy Sacrifice. Moreover, the conciliar decree *Religious Life* (25) desires that religious "love the Cross." If the People of God exercising the common priesthood of the faithful bestowed on them at Baptism are to offer themselves to God with Christ in the Eucharist, every more reason why religious who wish to live more fully their first consecration by the vows of religion must offer themselves in reparation to God.

Lastly, must one speak of radiating religious life? One simple sentence in the decree is sufficient to describe this: "The more ardently they unite themselves to Christ through a self-surrender involving their entire lives, the more vigorous becomes the life of the Church and the more abundantly her apostolate bears fruit" (1).

How many religious vocations came about because

the heart of a young man or a young woman had been charmed by the Heart of Christ! Attracted by the passionate love of this Heart, these young people wanted to please Him alone and repeat with St. Therese of Lisieux, "Thus, in my blissful joy, I cried out, 'O Jesus, my love, . . , my vocation, I have found it, my vocation is love!'"

Therefore, it should not be surprising to us that Jesus revealed His Heart to such consecrated souls as Gertrude, Mechtilda, Margaret Mary, Suso, and many others. It should not be surprising either that religious were the most ardent apostles of this Heart: Bonaventure, Foucauld, Father Mateo. Nor should it surprise us that so many religious congregations wanted to attach themselves to the Sacred Heart of Jesus by their name and spirit, and receive from this loving call "their way of life, their incentive for virtue, their motivation and the source of their missionary zeal."

May all consecrated souls and the religious families they belong to draw from the Heart of Jesus this "renewal of spirit" the council proposed to them. May their numbers multiply, their fervor deepen and expand, "for a more vigorous flowering of the Church's holiness and the greater glory of the one and undivided Trinity, which in Christ and through Christ is the fountain and the wellspring of all holiness!" (*Church*, 47).

CHAPTER SIX

THE PRIEST MODELED ON
THE HEART OF CHRIST

In the opening of the book of Samuel, the sacred writer tells us about the impostures and deceptions of the Sons of Elia, the high priest. Priests also, two scoundrels as the Bible tells us, they treated with disdain the offerings made to the Lord, usurping them. A man sent by God came to find the high priest and told him the chastisement of the Lord to punish his children. Then he added that the Lord said: "I will raise up a faithful priest for myself; he shall do whatever I plan and whatever I desire" (Is. 2:35).

For the People of God today, such a priest is as indispensable as during the time of Samuel. In examining the nature and the function of the Church, the Council could not omit the question of the priesthood. In the *Dogmatic Constitution on the Church*, the Church has already defined the place and the role of the priest in relation to the episcopate and the faithful. Nearly all the conciliar decrees have stressed in their subject matter the function of the priests.

Two decrees in particular, one on the formation of priests, the other on their life and ministry, have been consecrated to their mission in the Church. The doctrinal content of the latter document is complete and precise, notably in the first chapter which defines the nature of the presbytery and the condition of priests in the world. Some recent articles appearing in Catholic periodicals and reviews written by serious-minded religious priests have caused misunderstanding. For example, sentences like the following taken out of context: "A feeling of uselessness sometimes overtakes a priest, and he wonders what he can still do in the modern world" (cf. *Etudes*, June 1966).

In reviewing the decisions taken by the Council of Trent at the Counter-Reformation on the image and function of the "post-Tridentine" priest, the Church of Vatican II understands why the priests today feel somewhat forgotten in the matters treated by this Council. In its reaction against the Tridentine spirit, the Council has put less stress on the priest than on the People of God.   One question, however, cannot be omitted.   In this perspective, what does the "priestly vocation" mean?   Did the council documents not clarify the underlying restlessness of the priests who may be wondering if they would not have done more for God in the world as laymen?

The author of this treatise on *The Church and Love*, in reading the *Decree on the Ministry and Life of Priests*, is aware of the consideration and concern the conciliar Fathers gave the priest in presenting his life and ministry to evangelize the modern world.   In it, they retained the doctrine of the priestly function as it was clearly outlined by the Council of Trent.   Besides, the nature of the priesthood cannot be defined from the sociological point of view, in reference to a precise time or place, for the image of the world changes.   The nature of the priesthood is one with the Eternal Priesthood of Christ united to His infinite charity.   That is why with the Bishops of Vatican Council II we must study the real function of the priest, and who he is according to the Heart of Christ.   Indeed, the Heart of Christ sheds the ray of light--a priestly Heart, let us not forget--that shows the greatness of the person and work of the priest.

*   *   *

This same decree (2) reminds us that in Christ, "all the faithful are 'a chosen race, a royal priesthood.' They offer the spiritual sacrifices to God through Jesus Christ. (I Pet. 2:5). . .The same Lord has established certain ministers among the faithful in order to join them together in one body where 'all the members have not the same function' (Rom. 12:4). These ministers in the society of the faithful would be able by the sacred power of their order to offer sacrifice and to remit sins. They would perform their priestly office publicly for men in the name of Christ.

So it was that Christ sent the Apostles just as He Himself had been sent by the Father. Through these same apostles, He made their successors, the bishops, sharers in His consecration and mission. Their ministerial role has been handed down to priests in a limited degree. Thus established in the order of the priesthood, they are co-workers of the episcopal order in the proper fulfillment of the apostolic mission entrusted to the latter order by Christ."

The priest, then, is more than a baptized Christian, and his priesthood is different from that of the faithful and superior to it. The same conciliar decree (2) recalls that while the priesthood "presupposes the sacraments of Christian initiation, the sacerdotal office of priests is conferred by that special sacrament through which priests, by the anointing of the Holy Spirit, are marked with a special character and are so configured to Christ the Priest that they can act in the person of Christ the Head."

Therefore, the priest in the world today need not ask himself anxiously how he may serve the people. Modern times are not more pagan than the era of the apostles. Peter and Paul did not ask themselves so many questions. They simply went out to conquer the world, "appointed by God as a priest of Jesus Christ," said Paul (Rom. 15:16), "to carry out my priestly duty by bringing the 'Good News' from God to the Gentiles and so make them acceptable as an offering made holy by the Holy Spirit."

*   *   *

Sharing in the priesthood of Christ, the priests today, as in the past, have the same duties to fulfill. Their first duty in their ministry is to cooperate with the bishops, to proclaim the "Good News" of Christ to all men, "for through the saving Word the spark of faith is struck in the hearts of unbelievers, and fed in the hearts of the faithful. . . .No doubt, priestly preaching is often very difficult in the circumstances of the modern world. If it is to influence the mind of the listener more fruitfully, such preaching must not present God's Word in a general and abstract fashion only, but it must apply the perennial truths of the gospel to the concrete circumstances of life" (4).

In this first duty of his consecration, the priest already encounters the love of the Sacred Heart. In this Heart, the priest takes his courage to preach the Gospel in an authentic manner. "What is this message Christ, Pontiff and Sovereign Priest, gives to the world through his ministers participating in his priesthood?" he asks. Christ Himself gives the answer. It is His Gospel of love preached to the poor, in the biblical sense of the word, the poor in spirit, the humble and simple souls, hearts well-disposed, men of good will and God-fearing, waiting and preparing for the coming of his Kingdom.

It is this revelation of the love of the Invisible

Father who so loved the world and sent his only Son to care for fallen man, not to judge and condemn him but to save him. Saint Paul, priest and apostle of the New Testament in speaking of his new mission says: "I, who am less than the least of all the faithful, have been entrusted with this special grace not only of proclaiming to the Gentiles the infinite treasure of Christ, but also of explaining how the mystery is to be dispensed. Through all the ages, this has been kept hidden in God the creator of everything" (Eph. 3:8).

The priest of the New Law, therefore, is not the juridical guardian of morality, but a humble and patient teacher of souls, who initiates them in the school of the Sacred Heart, like St.John the Baptist, the precursor of Christ, who cried out to the people: "Behold the Lamb of God who takes away your sins." To all men who know not that Christ is love, the priest tries to teach them the knowledge that surpasses all other learning: the charity of Christ which fills souls with the fullness of God. Sin introduced in the world hatred and the refusal of Christ. The priest tells the world to look at the Heart of Christ that loves all men, and by this love to overcome hate.

In the language of love, Christ Himself speaks: "Fear not, little flock." This is the kingdom the Father prepares for us. Blessed, thrice blessed! Modeled on the Heart of Christ, the priest repeats the sermon on the Mount. Christ makes requests to be sure, but He promises more. He does not cry out: "Here is the anathema, the wrath of God! In a little while Niniveh will be destroyed." That was the voice of the prophet addressing itself to the People of God before Christ, to "hard headed nations with stiff necks."

Even today, hearts slow to believe still exist, but in Christ have appeared His divinity and humanity. He was not concerned with any righteous actions we might have done ourselves; it was for no reason except his own compassion that he saved us, by means of the cleansing water of rebirth and by renewing us with the Holy Spirit. This was the message of Christ, the Eternal priest. He does not cry out to the world condemnation for their sins, but as Saint Paul repeats in Christ, "This message of salvation is meant for you" (Acts 13:26).

The men today, like those of yesterday and tomorrow, listening to the language of love that understands weakness and even sin, of mercy and pardon, that gives compassion and saves, these men who feel abandoned and rejected suddenly discover they are the well-beloved of the Father, who has never ceased to cherish them, even in their unfaithfulness. Hearing the words of the Heart of Christ, they begin again to hope. Raising their eyes from the ground, they see on the mountain Him whom they pierced, their amazed but confident look penetrates the interior of the wounded side of Christ and they admit that this Man, who loved as no man ever before loved, is truly the Son of God.

The primary role of the priest is, then, to preach the Gospel of peace, the "Good News" of joy. He is the echo of the voice of Christ repeating his words of love, in the simple and direct language of Christ coming from the heart. To the modern world, the priest can say as St. Paul did to the Corinthians, "in my speeches and the sermons that I gave there were none of the arguments that belong to philosophy (I Cor. 2:4), but as we have the same spirit of faith that is mentioned in scripture: I believed, and therefore I spoke (II Cor. 4:13). . . ." In other words, God in Christ was reconciling the world to Himself, not holding men's faults against them, and He has entrusted to us the news that they are reconciled.   So we are ambassadors for Christ; it is as though God were appealing through us, and the appeal that we make in Christ's name is. "Be reconciled to God!"

*   *   *

The priest, become the shepherd of the flock, gathers then together in the name of the Good Shepherd and nourishes them.   The conciliar decree *Priests* (5) reminds us that "God, who alone is holy and bestows holiness, willed to raise up for Himself, as companions and helpers men who would humbly dedicate themselves to the work of sanctification. By baptism, men are brought into the People of God. By the sacrament of penance, sinners are reconciled to God and the Church. With the anointing of the sick, the suffering find relief. And especially by the celebration of Mass, men offer sacramentally the sacrifice of Christ."

The same decree continues (6): "As educators in the faith, priests must see to it, either by themselves or through others, that the faithful are led individually in the Holy Spirit to a development of their own vocation as required by the gospel, to a sincere and active charity, and to that freedom with which Christ has made us free." Priests belong to the people, but in a special way to the poor and the little ones, to the young, and also to the married people, to parents, to religious men and women, finally, to all sick and dying.

Thus, the priest is the pastor of souls that God spoke about in the Old Testament by the voice of Ezekiel, the prophet: "I shall withdraw my sheep from the shepherds who feed themselves? Shepherds ought to feed their flock, yet you have fed on milk, you have dressed yourselves in wools, you have sacrificed the fattest sheep. I am going to look after my flock myself and I mean to raise up one shepherd: he will pasture them and be their shepherd."

The priest must be a leader, not impose himself or dominate, but guide the People of God. He is their educator, protector and consoler. Like Christ he comforts souls: "That your heart may not be troubled!" He knows his sheep and loves them with the Heart of Christ. He seeks out the lost sheep and brings it back to the fold; if it is the victim of the devil's ruses, he takes it in and cares for it like the Good Samaritan. Christ put into his hands the power of mercy and pardon, so that he might have pity and forbearance.

In the fact of absolution he brings sinners to repentance; as another Christ he can cry out: "Today, salvation has come to this house!" Seeing the spiritual hunger the world is suffering from today, he proclaims the living Bread descended from heaven, prepares and distributes it. "I want my sheep to have life and have it more abundantly."

Above all, the priest is for souls the man of the Eucharist and the Mass, "for the most blessed Eucharist," says the above decree, "contains the Church's entire spiritual wealth, that is, Christ Himself, our Passover and living bread. Through His very flesh vivified by the Holy Spirit, He offers life to man. They are thereby invited and led to offer themselves, their labors and all created things together with Him. Hence the Eucharist shows itself to be the beginning and the end of the whole work of preaching the Gospel."

In the Eucharist, the ministry of the priest has its end; in it he finds fulfillment. For this ministry, which takes its start from the gospel message, derives its power and strength from the sacrifice of Christ. Its aim is that the entire commonwealth of the redeemed, that is, the community and society of the saints, be offered as a universal sacrifice to God through the High Priest who in His Passion offered Himself for us that we might be the body of so exalted a Head (2).

In accomplishing this supernatural task, the priest, another Christ, must not show preference: "Come to Me all of you," said the Master. In building the Christian Community, the priests are never to put themselves at the service of any ideology or human faction. With regard to all the faithful, in the name of charity and the supernatural maternity of the Church, he will repeat with Saint Paul: "My children, I must go through the pain of giving birth to you all over again, until Christ is formed in you" (Gal. 4:19). He will give witness to the Infinite tenderness of the Heart of Christ by confronting the world of sinners redeemed by His blood. He will manifest the passionate love with which Christ burns for all men: "this love is always patient and kind; it is never jealous; love is never boastful nor conceited. Love takes no pleasure in other people's sins but delights in the truth; it is always ready to excuse, to trust, to hope, and to endure whatever comes" (I Cor. 13:4-7).

Thus, witnesses of the Heart of Christ among men, heralds of the "Good News" and shepherds of the Church, they must devote themselves to the spiritual growth of the Mystical Body of Christ.

*   *   *

The sacerdotal tasks of the priest require more than simply human qualities.   The priest must strive for perfection in his ministry. As the Council reminds us of it: "In the consecration of baptism, like all Christians, they received the sign and the gift of so lofty a vocation and a grace that even despite human weakness they can and must pursue perfection according to the Lord's words: "You therefore are to be perfect, even as your heavenly Father is perfect" (Mt. 5:48).   "To the acquisition of this perfection, priests are bound by a special claim since they have been consecrated to God in a new way by the reception of orders. They have become living instruments of Christ the eternal priest, so that through the ages they can accomplish His wonderful work of reuniting the whole society of men with heavenly power.

Therefore, since every priest represents the person of Christ Himself, he is also enriched with special grace. Serving the people committed to him and the entire People of God, he can more properly imitate the perfection of Him Whose part he takes" (*Priests*, 12).

The sacerdotal vocation is a call to holiness. This holiness may be attained by the loyal and faithful exercise of their ministry in the spirit of Christ, for all priests the authentic means to arrive at sanctity, as the decree clearly states it.

What did Christ do? "He acted first and then taught," declares the Acts of the Apostles. He himself told us that he spoke from experience. "What we say, we know" (Jn. 3:11). The real priest, a mirror of the charity of Christ among the people, must witness Christ in words and actions. Having encountered and experienced Him, he can now speak of him. As Christ spoke to the Apostles, he speaks to them: "Henceforth, you shall be my friends, not my servants, for you know my secrets." By contemplating Christ on the cross, the priest puts his hand in the wound in Christ's side confirming his faith. Imploring the priest's

love, Jesus asks: "Do you love ME?   Do you love me
more than these?"   Then he answers, "Feed my lambs,
feed my sheep."

In the humility and meekness of the Sacred Heart,
the priest drinks from this fountain of eternal life before
leading others to the living waters that flow from this
pierced Heart.   By his chastity and purity of body and
heart, he follows the Lamb wherever He goes.   By his
intimacy with the Heart of Christ, he tries to vibrate His
same feelings, His same emotions, and His same anguishes.
He attempts to reproduce in himself the qualities of Christ.

Seeking to imitate Christ in all things, and manifest
his love among the people, the priest will also suffer a
wounded heart.   Taking up again the ritual of the priestly
ordination, the conciliar decree says: "As ministers of
sacred realities, especially in the sacrifice of the Mass,
priests represent the person of Christ in a special way.   He
gave Himself as victim to make men holy.   Hence priests
are invited to imitate the realities they deal with.   Since
they celebrate the mystery of the Lord's death, they should
see to it that every part of their being is dead to evil habits
and desires" (13).

This expression recalls the words of Saint John Bosco's mother, Margaret, when she spoke to her son the night of his ordination: "My child, to be ordained a priest and offer Mass is to begin to suffer." Just as Christ loved and sacrificed Himself for mankind, so must the priest love and sacrifice his time, health and very existence in apostolic tasks. Like Christ in Gethsemani, he must resist the power of darkness, fear and moral anguish in these days when faith seems lost; he must deliver himself to the calumny of false witnesses, the accusations of those whom he has helped and loved, the condemnation of his superiors when he was innocent. In short, he must surrender his heart to the lance that pierced the Heart of Christ. By these wounds, he is made whole in the Sacred Heart.

Some might say, this picture of the priesthood is mystical or idealistic. Not at all. Such priests do exist. Even if they do not all attain the ideal, they engage themselves with this intention in their ministry. To be sure, there was a traitor among the twelve apostles, a renegade and a deserter. Nevertheless there were eleven martyrs. "Can you drink the chalice I shall drink?" asked Jesus of the Sons of Zebedee whose mother asked that they sit, one on His right and the other on His left in His Kingdom.   James and John lovingly and spontaneously answered: "We can."   Jesus, looking through the veil of the future, knew they were speaking the truth: "Yes, you shall drink it!" he prophesied.

What priest today or in any era for that matter united intensely to the sacrifice of love on the cross for all men and for the glory of God, modeled on the Heart of Christ, could wonder if he is useless in the world in which he lives apart from everyone yet a brother to all?   The council and the Church of Vatican II have not misunderstood the role of the priest.   "The world," affirms the conciliar decree (22), "which is entrusted today to the loving ministry of the pastors of the Church is that world which God so loved that He gave His only Son for it."

The truth is that, though entangled indeed in many sins, this world provides the Church with the living stones which are to build the dwelling place of God in the Spirit. Priests should remember that in performing their tasks they are never alone.   Relying on the power of Almighty God and believing in Christ Who called them to share in His priesthood, they should devote themselves to their ministry with complete trust, knowing that God can intensify in them the ability to love.

     Heart of Jesus, sacerdotal heart of Christ,

     Raise up priests and sanctify them,

     Faithful priests, acting according to

     Your desires and your Heart!

CHAPTER SEVEN

THE HEART OF CHRIST
OPEN TO THE CHURCH

In its purpose, Vatican Council II set out to be preeminently pastoral. In a world of radical changes, rapidly losing spiritual values, it is necessary to present the real image of the Church and make known the message and spirit of the Gospel. Wishing to relate to the people of our times, the Church realized during Vatican II the hope the Council brought to the hearts of all men. The many problems today disturbing the minds and hearts of men remain without positive and authentic solutions. The threats weighing down on humanity, the sorrows that overwhelm it lead even the most estranged from the faith to look to Rome, to our Holy Father and the Church, as a call to Christ himself. Unconsciously, they cry out to him: "Lord, save us, we perish!"

In an effort to respond to the expectations of the world, the Council drew up the *Pastoral Constitution on the Church in the Modern World* to make known the Church to the men of our times.

From the beginning, receptive to human problems, the Church has always adapted herself to the needs of the times: for example, the Apostles were born in Judaism, yet knew how to turn courageously to the Gentiles. This same Church, in spite of persecutions, spread throughout the Roman Empire. In identifying itself with it, it strengthened civilization. Then, when the barbarian hordes, the Goths, Franks and the Alemanni, swept over the Old Roman Empire, leaving it devastated, and causing the Church much anxiety, Saint Augustine resolutely set out to evangelize them and conquer them for Christ. The examples throughout history are numerous. Today, in the young nations that gained independence, the Church continues to respect and esteem the people by giving them a clergy, bishops and even cardinals of their own race and nationality.

Should the openness and the receptivity of the Church still be questioned? Even in the early centuries, the

Church made use of Plato's philosophy to better interpret and present the doctrine of Christ. Nor did the Church with Saint Albert the Great and Saint Thomas Aquinas hesitate to use the philosophy of Aristotle and to Christianize it. In every age, the Church has been open also to the arts. They were not inhibited in the Christian cult any more than in the pagan Roman temple of Agrippa, or the Mosque of Cordova, as exemplified by the Gothic Cathedral of Reims, the baroque of Saint Peter's or the ultra-modern Cathedral of Brasilia. Likewise, the community of Christians identifies itself truly and intimately with mankind and its history. Indeed, nothing genuinely human fails to raise an echo in the heart of the followers of Christ.

Our purpose here is not to expound the long conciliar document, *The Church Today*, which has studied in detail the human conditions in today's world. But in keeping with it we must face the errors, the anguishes, doubts, aspirations and hopes of the world in which we live. The only valuable response to all these problems is the Incarnate Word, the God-Man, Jesus Christ. There can be no openness in the world without the Wounded Heart of

Christ, the Redeemer.

*   *   *

The world of today! What an exciting and at the same time discouraging spectacle it offers us! To be sure, it is neither better nor worse than in the centuries past. One finds in it the vision of the two infinities that the French writer Pascal discovered in man. Indeed, we are living in an era of continuous and radical changes, brought about by the discoveries of the human mind, but their rapid progression leaves man aghast, for he lives irrelevant to these changes. Hence social disturbances have come about; values are being questioned especially by the young. The norms of the past, and the manner of behavior and thinking no longer seem acceptable. While liturgy is strengthening the faith of some Christians, there is a noticeable loss of it in many others. The modern world might be characterized not only by the outward disorders from which it is suffering but also by the contradictions within the individual and within the family and social life which keep it divided.

Disorder in the personal life of individuals makes them unable to dominate and organize what they know.

They cannot combine expediency and the moral demands of their conscience. Nor can they escape the strains of modern living and develop their own personality by deepening it with interior silence. In the family, statistics show that tensions are created by economic problems, urban and inner city life, and the new relationship between the sexes.

In society, conflicts and misunderstandings are brought about by an overabundance of wealth, yet famine rages in many areas of the globe. The scientific achievements of some countries contrast with the high percentage of illiteracy elsewhere. A keen sense of personal freedom penetrates society while certain forms of social and psychological slavery overrun it. The consciousness of the oneness and solidarity of humanity is opposed to the political, social, racial, and ideological dissensions which threaten war. The search for truth and excellence by some in certain human organizations is overshadowed by the spiritual and moral decadence surrounding them.

Thus, *The Church Today* (9) states "the modern world shows itself at once powerful and weak, capable of the noblest deeds or the foulest. Before it lies the road to freedom or slavery, to progress or retreat, to brotherhood or hatred." Man is questioning himself. In truth, adds the text of the decree, the disorders in the world today are linked to a more fundamental disorder rooted in the heart of man. For in man himself, numerous elements are struggling with each other. "Thus, on the one hand, as a creature he experiences his limitations in a multitude of ways. On the other hand, he feels himself to be boundless in his desires and summoned to a higher life." In short, the division he suffers from in his own heart flows into the heart of society and creates in it great disorders. Thus man looks everywhere for solutions to liberate him of his interior confusion, solutions very human and inadequate.

The Conciliar Fathers affirm then: "The Church believes that Christ can through His spirit offer man the light and strength which allow him to measure up to his supreme destiny." Thus Christ Himself, human and divine, is the solution to the problems that torment the mind and heart of man. He is the "key, the focal point and the goal of all human history." The answer, therefore, to the unrest of the men of our times, as always, is Jesus Christ, in His passion, death and resurrection; His Heart opened by the lance of the soldier will remain open eternally to pour forth on all of us the abundance of His passionate love!

*   *   *

We must admit, then, that the troubles in the world today are due to the confusion that exists in the moral order. Only by returning to a true order of values can men eliminate the struggles, pains and anguishes of today's world. True order is not the materialism gaining control and dominating society. Neither can the syllogisms of thinkers, the inductions of the learned, the analogies of those who would like to be prophets satisfy the soul. "Insecurity forces man to think," says Albert Camus. Positive knowledge and learning alone cannot bring man peace of heart. In truth, what does all this knowledge count when compared with the science of Love, God Himself?

This God, however, is not distant and aloof. The true love He brings adapts to others, is warm, personal, intimate, reproducing in itself the creature loved. By love, His Son took on human flesh, became man, resembling us in all things but sin, and redeemed mankind of sin. This order of love originated in the human heart of Christ Who is infinite love. This divine love radiates and sheds itself to all men. It is this same love poured out on men that will in truth bring salvation again to the human race. No other heart can save it.

The Church, in opening itself up to the world, is again presenting to mankind the opened heart of the Redeemer. If man really wishes to be understood, he must penetrate this heart which loves him and possesses "all the treasures of wisdom and knowledge," inviting all: "Come to me, all of you!" If they have sinned, this open heart that Christ offers to His Father as their victim will be an abode of mercy and peace: "I am the resurrection and the life." If they still remain unbelieving, he will say to them, "Give me your hand; put it into my side. Doubt no longer, but believe" (Jn. 20:28-27.

The whole life of Christ here on earth was symbolized by the open wound in His heart embracing all men. He opens it to every individual and to the crowds who follow Him, whom He pities, to children, to the sick and the sorrowful, and to sinners. He cannot be indifferent to anything inhumane. On the contrary, everything touches

His heart and He is moved to action: the plea of the Centurion, the plight of the Canaanite woman, the sorrow of the widow of Naim, the death of Lazarus, Saint Peter's profession of faith, the love of James and John, the infidelity of Jerusalem, the betrayal of Judas. No human call echoed in His ear without affecting His heart: "Jesus, Son of David, have pity on me!. . . . Lord, if you had been here, my brother would not have died," and Christ responded with His love.

The miracles recounted in the Gospel stories are not prodigies of propaganda nor manifestations of power, but are essentially the testimony of the goodness of the Heart of Christ. His love endures and continues from century to century: the hope and refuge of man here below, His joy and glory for all eternity. Christ's Heart will remain open, not only to offer love to His Father, but to heap up treasures for the elect.

The answer of the Church to the men of our times, adapted to their aspirations, needs and suffering is found in the gospel, in the Heart of Christ. In *The Church Today*, the Church is aware that her message is in keeping with the profound desires of the human heart. Outside the Church, nothing can satisfy the heart. "You have made us for yourself, O Lord, and our heart knows no other respite, but what it finds in you."

Our Holy Mother, the Church, through Vatican Council II wishes to appear to all men as the irreproachable spouse of Christ. In this way, it can truly bring the essential response to the problems and questions of our times, alleviating human suffering. This human response of the Church is that of the Sacred Heart open to receive our pains and sorrows, hopes and joys, and even our sins. The world, besieged as it is by sin and suffering, is not shut out, for within the walls of the Church, so to speak, a door is open, allowing all men to enter where truth, liberty, the dignity of the human person, charity, peace and security reign. Through this open door, the flock of Christ will find green pastures and fresh water flowing from the Heart of Christ, always open to receive it.

CHAPTER EIGHT

FREEDOM IN THE HEART OF CHRIST

On December 7, 1965, the eve of the closing of Vatican Council II, Pope Paul VI promulgated the decree on *Religious Freedom*. It took the Conciliar Fathers two years from November 9, 1963 to the end of October 1965, to arrive at the definitive text of this document voted on by more than two thousand of them. The first schema had undergone six changes. As for the debates on this question, they aroused some of the most passionate controversies and polemics of the entire Council. Some feared that such a declaration would undermine the Catholic faith in the one true Church, stir up a crisis on authority in the Church, teach religious indifferentism and relativism. Others were equally concerned with defending the notion of the Catholic State, one of whose functions, in the name of the common good, is the repression of heresy.

In speaking of religious freedom, does not this declaration admit that truth can be multiple and exist apart from Christ, that the Catholic Church is not the true Church, and that everyone need not be subject to Christ, the Redeemer, in whom is all primacy? Would not such a decree be in contradiction to the condemnations brought about by the Church in the nineteenth century? Would it not yield to the more or less reasonable desire for independence and freedom of conscience filling the heart of modern man, conceding in the long run to a free and easy conception of ecumenism not well understood?

It is clear, therefore, why the debates were long, arduous and sometimes vehement, much more as told in certain newspapers and magazines than actually in the conciliar Aula of Saint Peter's Basilica. One must admit the problems were different in the various countries from which the Bishops came. Their experience depended on whether or not religious freedom had been meaningful in those countries. This experience naturally gave rise to the different points of view held by the Bishops which biased news commentators presented as fiercely opposed to each other.

Nevertheless, the Church, wanting to convey its message to the modern world, open itself to it and return to the Gospel teachings of Christ, voted and promulgated this rich and valuable decree on religious freedom, defining it with clarity and basing it on Sacred Scripture itself. As Cardinal König wrote: "This document constitutes a remarkable and important event in the history of the Church, capable of opening a new era in the relationship of the Church with the modern world."

This document makes known Christ's love for all men guaranteeing them liberty of conscience, freeing them from all exterior and interior constraints. By His own example He merited it for mankind. What human heart loved with more freedom than the Heart of the God-Man? In this freedom, we can respond more fully to Christ's invitation: "Come, learn of Me," in the school of His Heart.

* * *

At the beginning of the conciliar document, an important fact was asserted: the modern world's consciousness of the dignity of the human person. Man aspires today to act according to his own desires, to become involved in society with full responsibility. The Conciliar Fathers assert also that God Himself made known to mankind the way men are to serve Him and thus be saved in Christ and come to blessedness.

To the Catholic and Apostolic Church, God gave the commandment to spread the true religion among men. Do these two ideas oppose each other? The Conciliar Fathers answer: "The truth cannot impose itself except by virtue of its own truth, which penetrates the spirit at once quietly and with power." The Vatican Council declares that every person has a right to religious freedom. This term must be well understood. It is not a question here of interior freedom, the power of free choice of the will to decide between two or more options presenting themselves.

On the contrary, it is a matter of freedom of exterior constraint: "All men," says the decree (2), "must be immune from coercion on the part of individuals or of social groups and any human power, in such a way that in matters religious no one is to be forced to act in a manner contrary to his own beliefs. Nor is anyone to be restrained from acting in accordance with his own beliefs, privately or publicly, whether alone or in association with others, within due limits. [This] right of religious freedom has its foundation in the very dignity of the human person, as this dignity is known through the revealed Word of God and by reason itself. This right of the human person to religious freedom is to be recognized in the constitutional law whereby society is governed. Thus, it is to become a civil right."

The highest norm in man's life is the divine law, eternal, objective and universal. Man has been made by God to participate in this law. Hence every man has the duty, and therefore the right, to seek the truth in matters religious. Thus a person cannot be coerced, or restrained to act in a manner contrary to his conscience, especially in religious matters, for, we recall the words of the declaration: "of its very nature the exercise of religion consists before all else in those internal, voluntary and free acts whereby man sets the course of his life directly to God. No merely human power can either command or prohibit acts of this kind. Injury, therefore, is done to the human person and to the very order established by God for human life, if the free exercise of religion is denied in society when the just requirements of public order do not so require" (3).

The declaration considers next the freedom of religious groups. The social nature of man itself requires that he should give external expression to his internal acts of religion. It treats of religious freedom in the family, notably in the matter of education, and the responsibilities of individuals, social groups, and public powers, as well as the Church and religious freedom and its training in the use of freedom which is not a rejection of all submission and the refusal of obedience.

In the second part of the declaration, the Council studies religious freedom in the light of Revelation. Respect for religious freedom rises out of a consciousness of the dignity of the human person. The act of faith is of its very nature a free act. The teaching of Christ, the Apostles, the Church, all affirm the right of religious freedom. There were, to be sure, in the life of the People of God, through the vicissitudes of human history, ways of acting less conformable, even contrary to the evangelical spirit. "Nevertheless, the doctrine of the Church, that no one can be coerced in the faith, has always stood firm" (12). It is, moreover, thus that "in human society and in the face of government, the Church claims freedom for herself in her character as the spiritual authority established by Christ the Lord. Upon this authority there rests, by divine mandate, the duty of going out into the whole world and preaching the gospel to every creature" (13).

Acknowledging that all nations today are coming into closer unity, men of different cultures and religions are being brought together in closer relationship, there is a growing consciousness of the personal responsibility that weighs upon every man (15). The declaration concludes thus: "In order that relationships of peace and harmony may be established and maintained within the whole of mankind, it is necessary that religious freedom be everywhere provided with an effective constitutional guarantee, and that respect be shown for the high duty and right of a man freely to lead his religious life in society" (15).

This declaration merely exposes the traditional teaching of the Church throughout the centuries. Its public affirmation by the council does not constitute less a condemnation of certain actions of the past, such as the recourse to power or religious wars, the intolerance manifested by some nations or social orders, officially professing a certain religion or even atheism. It is a vigorous defense against all those who would want to oppress the right of conscience. By it, the Conciliar Fathers clearly brought out before the eyes of the world the doctrine of the Church, and forcefully affirmed it to all individuals or groups wishing to pressure the souls of men. *The Declaration on Religious Freedom* is, then, both a profession of faith and an act of courage.

*   *   *

In all of this, devotion to the Heart of Christ is not a simple act of piety or even a reparation of love, but rather the contemplation of a model, the education of the soul by a Master, in imitation of Him, of His love and sentiments. Real devotion to the Sacred heart is, indeed, the exchange of our heart with His, conformity to its views and interests, the perfect union of our wills. In this heart which burns for all mankind is the devotion He came to establish in spirit and in truth. He embraces all men of good will with understanding affection.

Christ did not come to abolish the Old Testament, but to fulfill the Law, not omitting even the least *iota*. In the letter of the law which kills, He wishes to substitute the spirit to give it life. He refuses lip service and purely legalistic sacrifices, requires an interior sanctity that alone can honor the Father in Heaven. There is nothing more revolutionary when we think of the Sermon on the Mount in reference to the Law of Moses and the Prophets, the controversies of the Pharisees in Jerusalem and St. John's account ending in the admirable discourse of the Last Supper in which Christ gave his disciples the new commandment of the Christians: brotherly love, in imitation of His Heart. This love must consequently give witness in the heroism of the bloody sacrifice of one's life.

In place of the simple external actions imposed by the tradition of the ancients, Christ instituted purity of Heart that alone fulfills the law of God. "To eat, with unwashed hands," He said one day, "does not make a man unclean. But the things that come out of the mouth come from the heart, and it is these that make a man unclean. For from the heart come evil intentions; murder, adultery, fornication, theft, perjury, slander" (Mt. 15:18-20). He declares also: "You have learned how it was said, 'You must not commit adultery.' But I say this to you: if a man looks at a woman lustfully, he has already committed adultery with her in his heart" (Mt. 11:27-28). "You have learned how it was said" 'You must love your neighbor and hate your enemy.' But I say this to you: 'Love your enemies'" (Mt. 5:42). "When you give alms. . .and when you pray. . .when you fast, do it in secret. And your Father who sees all that is done in secret will reward you."

The interior religion of love preached by Christ is not one of social restraints, either traditional or racial, nor is it legalistic, imposed by texts or rabbinical jurisprudence, but one lived in complete freedom. Jesus wishes to draw us to Himself in grace and in loving invitation: "Come, follow me." In his commands, Christ uses the language of love and freedom: "If you wish to be perfect, sell what you have, give to the poor and follow Me!"; again, "If anyone is thirsty, let Him come to Me!" "If any one will come after Me, let him take up his Cross!" Raised above the earth, he will draw all things to Himself, not force them. He wishes to be followed, not by necessity, but by love, which presupposes freedom. "The sheep that belong to me listen to my voice; I know them and they follow Me" (Jn. 10:27).

One discovers in these words of Christ all the spontaneity of love and attachment found in the Heart of Christ for all mankind. Christianity is only the recognition of the generous love and heart of Christ to whom we have confided ourselves and who first loved us. In this personal relationship existing between the God-Man and His creatures, the Christian faith demands absolute freedom.

Wishing to set the world on fire with this religion of love, totally intimate and sincere, the love of God united with the love of man, Christ met hostility, intolerance, and wickedness at the hands of the Pharisees. Representing the official religion, they imposed on each other the burden of sectarianism; not bearing it themselves, they were hypocrites, blind men leading other blind men to the grave, closing thus the kingdom of heaven to all men. They could not accept a Gospel completely authentic and loyal, having no other goal than the freedom of the soul to abandon itself to God.

Simplicity, naturalness, candor in the relationship of man with God, of Christ with His Father, all of that scandalized these narrow minds filled with conceit and ready to make others bend under their totalitarian authoritarianism. They set snares for Christ, tried to trap Him, asked insidious questions, stoned Him, and cast out of the synagogue those who believed in Him. But Jesus confounded them: "God knows your hearts. They are loathsome in his sight" (Lk. 16:15). Their fanatic pride, however, ended in seizing Christ. They condemned Him to death, accusing Him of blasphemy. "He tried to make himself the Son of God." Christ told them His freedom would dominate their violence: "My life no man takes away from me, but it is I who give it" (Jn. 10:18).

Towards the pagans, unbelievers and even heretics, the Savior acts only according to the dictates of His Heart. For the Centurion and the Canaanite Woman who manifested such faith in Him, Christ openly expresses His admiration and works great miracles. In the case of the Samaritan woman, a sinner, Jesus, knowing her interests and aspirations, raised her to the spiritual heights of true adoration and love. When the Samaritans badly received Christ, and the Sons of Zebedee complained against them, the Savior replied: "You know not what spirit you are!" When someone not a disciple of Christ tried to cast out demons, in the name of Jesus, the disciples, seeing this, tried to prevent him, 'because he is not with us,' they said. But our Lord answered: "Do not hinder him, for he who is not against us is for us."

This tolerance of Christ in no way indicated timidity on His part to affirm the truth. Quite the contrary. Jesus dialogued with the Pharisees, enlightened Nicodemus, did not refuse explanations to Pilate, for in this cowardly Roman magistrate afraid of the people He recognized sincerity. Whether Christ speaks with the authority of His Father or protects those not with Him, it is always with the language of love: "Come to Me! Learn of Me, for I am meek and humble of Heart!" In respecting the conscience of all men, He declares unforgivable only the sin against the Holy Spirit. Christ calls His sheep to the fold not by the strokes of the staff but by His gentle voice. He brings back the lost sheep joyously on His shoulder recalling the words of St. Augustine: "We attract the sheep with the green palm that we offer him; we attract a child with nutmeats." The real act of faith based on absolute freedom is the same that attracts the heart of man to the Heart of Jesus Christ.

*   *   *

True freedom, then, is freedom of spirit, detached from its interior slavery and its passions. The worst religious intolerance does not come from coercion, but from the evil within ourselves. Martyrs, for example, tortured for the faith, died resisting violence, and even triumphed over it, while sinners in an encounter with their conscience deliberately choose to do evil and reject what is good. Thus, conscience declares its absolute autonomy.

As Gustav Thibon says of the sinner: "He escapes the authority of things above that nourish him, only to fall into the tyranny of things below that devour him." By putting himself in opposition to the law of God, truth and good, he provokes within himself discord, division, and anguish. Casting aside the best for the worst, real happiness for foolish pleasures, he falls into slavery, feeling degraded and dishonored. Trying to free himself from this slavery and the remorse of his conscience, he only falls back into selfishness and deception. In this traumatic experience, the sinner refuses God, and sacrifices himself to his own idol. He outrages his reason, falls short of attaining his manhood and commits a violation against his will.

Christ came upon earth precisely to restore to man the real meaning of interior freedom, and especially to merit for sinful humanity freedom from the slavery of evil. True freedom for a disciple of Christ, in imitation of his Master, is not only conformity to the will of His heavenly Father, but the abandonment of Himself to His love. This filial submission Christ taught by His example and by His preaching when He said: "I come, O Lord, to do your will. . . ." At the passion, He repeats: "Not my will, but yours be done!" The Christian assumes the personality of Christ by doing His divine will and develops it in His love, not as a slave, but as a Son. "I wish only the will of him who possesses me; that is all," says Paul Claudel. In this way, he possesses the freedom of the children of God.

In order to restore this freedom and divine adoption Christ redeemed mankind with His blood. "God loved us with so much love that He was generous with His mercy. When we were dead through our sins, he brought us to life with Christ" (Eph. 2:4-5). Again, we became Sons of God and heirs of His kingdom, called to Freedom (Gal. 5:13), restored in Christ Jesus (Gal. 4:31). In our soul, the spirit of the Lord echoes in us with love: "Father! Father!" Saint

Paul adds, "Where the spirit of the Lord is, there is freedom" (II Cor. 3:17). Did not Christ Himself say: "I tell you most solemnly every one who commits sin is a slave. . .So, if the Son makes you free, you will be freed indeed" (Jn. 8:34, 36). Such is the liberty Christ gained for us on the cross.

The religious freedom which the conciliar decree speaks of is only "a participation analogical to the freedom of the Christian, found in baptismal grace and in the gift of the Holy Spirit," as Cardinal König explained. Both were willed for us by the loving Heart of our Savior. In this, He wished to obtain the free return of man's love that it may become one with His Heart. This Heart wishes only absolute good; he loves and chooses only God, the Father, who gave him all and to whom he wishes to restore all things, in particular the lost children, whom He came to seek and to save. His meat, then, is to accomplish the will of the Father, to be his servant, and even the servant of His brethren, washing their feet as He did those of the Apostles at the Last Supper.

The Heart of Christ, therefore, is a free and loving Heart, a filial Heart obedient even to the death of the cross.

In this Heart which loved men so much, the beautiful description of Paul Claudel in *Tidings Brought to Mary*, takes meaning:

> The Cross . . .
>
> Not to live, but to die
>
> Not to frame
>
> But to ascend.
>
> Give all laughing . . .
>
> Joy
>
> Freedom.

Our heart, too, will be full when it goes all the way by love to the Father, like the Heart of Jesus Christ!

CHAPTER NINE

MARY THE MOTHER OF THE CHURCH

The Ecumenical Council Vatican II has openly manifested the mystery of the Church, the mystical Body of Jesus Christ. In the eyes of Christians, it has revealed the true image of the Spouse of Christ.

The Conciliar Fathers, guided by the Holy Spirit in defining the nature and role of the Church, have by this very fact given witness to the person and function of Mary, her Mother and Spouse. In chapter eight of *The Church*, the Council speaks of the Blessed Virgin Mary, Mother of God, placing her within the mystery of Christ and the Church. "The Church," Bossuet tells us, "is Jesus Christ diffused and communicated in his fullness."

How could we then receive the love that comes from Christ's Heart, if not in the same way Mary received it into her own heart? How could we receive it, if it were not transmitted through her maternal intercession, since she is the Spouse of Christ and Mother of the Church? To say we go to the Heart of Christ through the Heart of Mary is not a figure of speech or an oratorical banality. Rather, this expression conveys an authentic supernatural reality. We shall prove it by first considering the Immaculate Heart of Mary, as a model of the Church, fashioned on the Heart of Christ and filled with his grace, and secondly, by contemplating the heart of the Virgin Mother completely devoted to the Heart of Christ filling souls with his love.

*   *   *

According to Genesis, the first Eve, the mother of the human race, was created by God from the side of the first Adam whom God also created in the beginning. The new Eve, the Church, mother of all those who are born of God and who live in Him, came forth mystically from the wounded side of Jesus Christ, the new Adam. In the blood mixed with water that flowed from the sacred wound of the sacrificial Lamb, sinful humanity, the daughter of anger, again became the daughter of Sion, a redeemed people, a saintly, royal and priestly nation.

The birth of the Church is the very manifestation of

the tenderness of God for men, of his redeeming love. "Christ loved the Church," proclaimed Saint Paul to the Ephesians (5:25-26), "and He delivered Himself for it, in order to sanctify it while purifying it by the bath of water that a word accompanied." "Christ Jesus," the same apostle said to Titus (2:14), "sacrificed himself for us in order to set us free from all wickedness and to purify a people so that it could be his very own and would have no ambition except to do good."

In relating the episode of the stroke of Longinus' lance in the Heart of the Savior, Saint John recalled the words of the prophet Zachariah: "They looked upon him whom they pierced." In some verses that followed, the prophet states even the effects of Christ's wound: "When that day comes, a fountain will be opened for the House of David and the citizens of Jerusalem, for sin and impurity" (Zach. 13:1).

In fact, Saint Paul added: "The Savior wanted to present his Church to himself, glorious with no speck or wrinkle, or anything like that but holy and faultless" (Eph. 5:27). Likewise, the Apostle Peter teaches (I Pet. 1:3-4) that God "in his great mercy has given us a new birth. .

and the promise of an inheritance that can never be spoiled or soiled and never fade away."

This purifying of sinful humanity was effected by the blood and the love of the Heart of Jesus Christ. It is an act of mercy, of infinite charity and of tender love. From his open Heart, this Savior allows to flow on humanity "peace, like a river" (Is. 46:12). In spite of its numerous sins, Christ loved this humanity the prophets called the "adulterous unfaithful spouse." He, however, came back to her and spoke to her in His Heart, so that she answers Him as in the days of her youth (Hos. 1), when man had not yet sinned. When He pardons, when He wishes to reestablish the union broken by so much refusal of love, He uses the language of affection. "I shall betroth you to myself forever, betroth you with integrity and justice, with tenderness and love; I will betroth you to myself with faithfulness" (Hos. 21:25).

Therefore, since Christ loves sinful humanity so much as to shed His blood, the wound in His side becomes then "the Jerusalem coming down from God out of heaven, as beautiful as a bride all dressed for her husband. . .Here God lives among men. He will make his home among them; they shall be his people, and he will be their God; his name is God-with-them" (Rev. 21:3).

When the Heart of Christ loved the Church and delivered itself for it to purify it and make it holy, did not this same love make the heart of Mary pure and immaculate? If we consider the Virgin Mary, the model of the Church, we shall not be surprised at the privilege of her Immaculate Conception. The Church was purified from sin, but Mary was preserved from it. Only the application of the merits of the redemption varies.

In both cases, Christ loved and delivered Himself; the same blood flowed from His pierced side, the same love flowed from His Heart, the river of living water, limpid, crystal, silent from the Heart of the immolated Lamb, from the wound in the right side of the Holy Temple of God. But if this living source brings humanity to life again from its dead works, it waters a heart that no evil barrenness has withered, or sterilized; without first healing, it gives growth to life wherever it flows.

Mary, like the Church, is without "speck or wrinkle, or anything like that" (Eph. 5:27), but also holy, pure and full of grace. The love of God sanctified her in preserving her from all sin, as it purified the Church of all sin. So that Mary might love the Church, God first loved her freely and magnificently, offered her His loving Heart through Christ in whom all tends to God and His glory, a selfless Heart, filled with pure love, which knew no sin, participating in the "eternal childhood of God," born in innocence and peace, overflowing with the infinite treasures of God's love.

In the measure in which God's love bore fruit in her, Christ continued to bless her and embrace her in the fullness of His love. Choosing her for His Mother, Christ filled the heart of Mary through the Holy Spirit given to her with His grace, "the free gift of being made righteous" (Rom. 5:17). In this way, the Son of God Himself, by the privilege He bestowed on His Mother, prepared His Church. Mary would be its loving model, and perfect symbol; her holiness would be the example of holiness restored to the Church by the love of the Heart of Christ.

In his discourse on June 15, 1966, Our Holy Father Pope Paul VI stated: "The supreme love of Christ for His Church can be compared to a human marriage in the natural order, though His love is much deeper and more meaningful." "This allegory," adds Our Holy Father, "teaches us the intimate and indissoluble union that exists between Christ and His Church, and at the same time the distinction between them." The Church is Christ. From Him, it receives its dignity, its sanctifying power, its humble yet royal origin. It is not only a means of salvation, but through it the Lord accomplishes His design of love, the mystery of charity, the love of the world and humanity, in the Holy Spirit.

This love which the Church receives from the open Heart of Christ, His faithful spouse, the Church attempts to give back to Him. She contemplates Him, Who was pierced for her and gave her birth. As the apostle asks: Does she not lose sight of Jesus who leads us in our faith and brings it to perfection; "for the sake of the joy that was still in the future, he endured the cross" (Hebr. 12:2). With all the faithful, she tries to understand the dimension of the love of God in the Heart of Christ. She meditates the marvels of God's mercy toward her, and in the Holy Spirit, she calls Christ who has chosen her as spouse: "Amen: come, Lord Jesus!" (Rev. 22:20). Looking on Him, she tries to imitate Him, to reproduce His image, His feelings, His divine will, His meek and humble Heart. As a wife toward her husband, the Church submits to Christ, the Head and Lord of the mystical Body. United to Christ in the same way as Christ is one with His Father, the Church accepts and does His will, giving witness of her union with Him.

By His blood, Christ saved all men, making them children of God and of the Church. As Saint Ambrose said: "The Church is the Mother of the living," and Bossuet spoke out: "The Title of Spouse was necessary to make the Church appear as the faithful companion of Jesus Christ, the dispenser of His grace, the directress of His family, the fruitful Mother and nurse always faithful to all her children. . .The church in its unity and universal spirit is the Mother of all men who compose the Body of the Church. She makes them children of Christ, not in the way of other mothers, in her own body, but in bringing them to Herself from without."

Pope Paul VI declared, also, "The Church is our mother; we give all to her. She gave us new life, in the life of grace. She gave us faith; by her teaching, she preserves it for us intact and fruitful. She gave us the sacraments, guides us, defends us, leads us to hope, the desire of eternal life, and a foretaste of happiness with her." The Church gives witness to Christ by the love she bears Him, in return for His love, in her supernatural motherhood. Was it for this reason that Christ chose her for His well-beloved spouse?

"Blessed," said Christ, "are they who hear the word of God and keep it." The Virgin Mary, above all others, not only listened to the Word of God, but she profoundly accomplished His will. This Eternal Word took flesh in her and became Man. *The Church* declares. . . "Mary received the Word of God in her heart and in her body, and gave Life to the World (53). . .By consenting to the divine utterance, Mary, a daughter of Adam, became the Mother of Jesus. Embracing God's saving will with a full heart and impeded by no sin, she dedicated herself totally as a handmaid of the Lord to the person and work of her Son. In subordination to Him and along with Him, by the grace of almighty God, she served the mystery of redemption" (56). Therefore, Mary, the spouse of the Mystical Christ, became the Mother of the Church.

Giving witness to Christ, contemplating His

miracles in faith, she kept all these things in her heart. During His hidden and public life, she looked silently and adoringly on His action. On Calvary, she stood at the foot of the cross, assisted at the last agony and death of her eternal Son; she watched the soldier pierce his Heart with a lance; she realized His hour had come, not to show His power but His love and mercy. She looked on Christ's open side, and entered in spirit into this Temple of God, the Holy of Holies from which flowed out blood and water. This model of faith in the Heart of Christ is Mary at Golgotha.

On Calvary, she is not merely a witness. She is coredemptrix. As always, servant of the Lord and subject to His divine will of love, the new Eve is completely united to the obedience of the new Adam. Together they restore divine life in the world. At the Annunciation, she is already Mother of the Mystical Body. She officially becomes so at the foot of the cross. "Mary, Mother of the Incarnate Word," said Pope Paul, "is, by the divine plan, equally the spiritual Mother of humanity; she wept and suffered for us," the souls Christ redeemed. "The maternal duty of Mary toward men in no way obscures or diminishes this unique mediation of Christ, but rather shows its power," states *The Church* (60).

Mary at the Cross is Mother of the Church. By her sorrow and loving obedience, she fulfills what is lacking in the passion of Christ for His Mystical Body, the Church. Her action does not end on Good Friday night: "For, taken up to heaven, she did not lay aside this saving role, but by her manifold acts of intercession continues to win for us gifts of eternal salvation. . . .By her maternal charity, Mary cares for the brethren of her Son, who still journey on earth surrounded by dangers and difficulties until they are led to their happy fatherland" (62).

As Saint John Eudes has written: "The Heart of Mary cooperates with the Heart of her Son Jesus in his work. . .in distributing to man with great charity the fruits of His life, passion, and death, the graces and blessings he merited for them during his mortal life, whose maternal heart is the depository and guardian."

Through this spiritual Motherhood of humanity, the heart of Mary returns this love to the Son of God who has given her all tenderness. With Christ, she penetrates the deepest mystery hidden in God for centuries, to know the merciful redemption of man, its original purity and restoration of its primary dignity as spouse of the Lord. Thanks to Mary, Christ can dwell in our hearts through faith. Her maternity permits us to be rooted in love, to know the charity of Christ which surpasses all knowledge and be filled with God himself.

Mary, model of the Church, has received all things from the Heart of the Son of God. As Mother of the Church, she returns all through love. She listens with favor to the Heart of Christ to save souls from death and to feed them in their hunger. She works untiringly to bring them to the Redeemer to embrace in his Heart that He may love them more and more, and they may love Him in return.

Children of Mary and of the Church, beneficiaries of this two-fold maternity we receive through all the gifts of the love of the Heart of Jesus grace upon grace. Like Mary, like the Church, we can say: "He loved me and delivered Himself for me!" Mary, model of the Church, asks us also to make our lives a perpetual act of thanksgiving to God Who first loved us, remembering His mercy and showering us with His goodness.

As Mother of the Church, she shows us also how to answer the loving charity of Christ. Having received the Word of God, having meditated on it in prayer, we shall preserve it only by obedience to the will of Christ. We shall then witness the love of God, the Father, and Christ, the Heart, sharing in this way the supernatural motherhood of Mary and the Church, shedding about us the love of Christ. He who does not really love cannot communicate Love. In the example of Our Lady, Mother of the Church, may our love of the Heart of Jesus become effective, a love in keeping with the teachings of Pope Paul VI in his allocution of November 6, 1964, which will engender concrete works to extend the kingdom of the love of Christ on earth.

PART II

AN EPILOGUE

*POPE JOHN PAUL II AND THE
DEVOTION TO
THE SACRED HEART OF JESUS*

I

The personal devotion of His Holiness John Paul II, lover of the Sacred Heart of Jesus, dates from his boyhood, and has continued to the present. Even before he was elected Pope, as Cardinal Archbishop of Krakow, in a pastoral letter written June 11, 1965 to commemorate the two hundredth anniversary of the establishment of the *Feast of the Sacred Heart of Jesus* which was celebrated first in Poland, he referred to the Litany of the Sacred Heart quoting what soon became his favorite invocation, "Heart of Jesus, fountain of life and holiness."

On June 20, 1979, during his first year as Pope, while celebrating the feast of the *Solemnity of the Sacred Heart of Jesus* in a general audience, he spoke these words: "Let us learn to meditate on the mystery of the Heart of Jesus; the Litany is full of the riches of His Heart. Let us attentively meditate on them today."

In his first encyclical letter as Pope, referring to the Eucharist, he again quoted his favorite invocation: "Fountain of life and holiness," and gave as his source the Litany of the Sacred Heart of Jesus.

On various occasions and under differing

circumstances, His Holiness commented frequently on many aspects of the mystery of Christ's love under the symbolism of His Heart. He not only advocated praying the Litany of the Sacred Heart, but also in his words: "reciting, singing and above all meditating on it." He especially encouraged his audience to meditate on it during June, the month dedicated to the Sacred Heart of Jesus when the Church placed before us the mysteries of the *Heart of Jesus*, the God-man.

Occasionally, Pope John Paul II also referred to the *Jesus Prayer*, a form traditionally practiced in Eastern spirituality, especially Russian. This prayer must come from the heart; "in the heart is life," he said. One must learn to pray, "heart speaking to heart, breathing and praying the name of *Jesus, the prayer of Jesus, the Heart of Jesus.*"

On July 1, 1984, in an Angelus message delivered from the Vatican at mid-day on Sunday, he spoke on the Heart of Christ, saying, "In the Heart of Christ there is a synthesis of all the mysteries of our faith," and again advocated praying the Litany and meditating on the invocations. These traditional practices invite the people of

God to recognize the treasures of the Heart of Jesus.

Invocations may be used also as one's personalized form of the *Jesus Prayer*, for example, "Heart of Jesus, our life and resurrection, have mercy on me." The invocation may be shortened to fit individual spiritual needs or preferences, as for instance, "Lord Jesus, have mercy on me." When the Litany is prayed together by a group, the response may be, "Lord Jesus, have mercy on us."

At times, Pope John Paul II in his meditations referred to the scriptural sources and the biblical phrases of the invocations as a stimulus to others to meditate on the Heart of Jesus more fruitfully. The examples that follow are excerpts taken from his *Angelus Meditations on the Litany of the Sacred Heart of Jesus*.

In meditating on the invocation: "Heart of Jesus, fountain of life and holiness," His Holiness recalled the incident when Jesus went to the village of Samaria, in Sichar, and met there a Samaritan woman who had come to draw water from Jacob's well. He said to her: "Give me a drink." The woman replied: "How is it that you, a Jew, ask a drink of me, a woman of Samaria?" Then Jesus replied: "If you knew the gift of God and who it is saying to you 'Give me a drink,' you would have asked him, and he would have given you living water." He continued: "The water that I shall give will become a spring of water welling up to eternal life." Our Holy Father then quoted the biblical reference (John 4:5-14) To conclude, he asked the Mother of Christ to be our guide to the Heart of her son.

Again, while meditating on the invocation: "Heart of Jesus, our peace and reconciliation," Our Holy Father explained that Jesus is our "peace." In the biblical sense of the word, peace signifies the sum total of the "good" which Jesus, the Messiah, has brought to humanity. It constitutes the crowning glory of His mission on earth. "Peace: Angels singing near the crib of the newborn "Prince of Peace." (Luke 2:14; Isaiah 9:5) "Peace is the greeting that springs from the Heart of Christ, moved to pity by the pain of a person who is suffering physically" (Luke 8:48) or "spiritually" (Luke 7:50). "Peace is the shining greeting of the risen Christ to his disciples" (Luke 24:36; John 20:19,26), to whom, when at the hour in which he would leave this earth, he entrusted the action of the Holy Spirit, fountain of "love, joy and peace"

(Galatians 5:22).

Our Holy Father then concluded with this prayer to Our Lady: "May Mary, Queen of Peace, obtain for us from Christ the messianic gift of peace and the grace of full and lasting reconciliation with God, and with our brothers and sisters. For this, let us pray."

In his meditation on the invocation: "Heart of Jesus, pierced with a lance," Pope John Paul II spoke on the attention given to this passage from St. John's Gospel, more than any other, by mystics, spiritual writers and theologians. It describes Christ's glorious death and the piercing of his side (19:23-27). His Holiness contemplates the filial obedience of Jesus to the Father whose task he courageously fulfilled (John 9:30) and his fraternal love for man whom He loved to the end (John 13:1), to the ultimate sacrifice of Himself. "Beside the cross was Mary, the Mother of Jesus." (John 19:25)

No sooner had the soldier struck the blow with the lance, than "there came out blood and water" from Christ's wounded side (John 19:34). The blow of the lance established the fact of Christ's death. "He is truly dead, as he was truly born, and as he would truly rise again in His own body (John 20:24-27)." In this passage, the Evangelist, John, clearly emphasizes Christ's death and His return to life in the Resurrection. His Holiness Pope John Paul II concluded this meditation by asking Mary to lead us to draw more and more abundantly from the streams of grace flowing from Christ's wounded heart.

In November of 1989, Pope John Paul II completed a series of Sunday Angelus messages begun in 1985, the longest series thus far devoted to a single subject: *The Litany of the Sacred Heart of Jesus.* These messages have a clear reference to the mystery of the incarnation and to Mary, the Mother of God who leads us to the Heart of her Son, the God man.

Prior to the above date, on June 27, 1982, Our Holy Father had devoted a Sunday Angelus message to a reflection on the Litany of the Sacred Heart and quoted seven of its thirty-three invocations. Although this message is not one of the series of meditations, it is included in this collection as the first of the Angelus messages on the Litany. After the summer of 1986, they were interrupted for themes dealing with the Marian Year 1987-1988.

Reflections on the Sacred Heart were resumed with

nine talks from July to September of 1989 and were concluded with the two final Angelus messages during November 1989, as stated above.

On the occasion of the third centenary of the death of Saint Margaret Mary, the Visitandine at Paray-le-Monial, France, to whom the Lord Jesus had appeared and entrusted with these striking and startling words: "Behold this heart which has so loved human beings and which has spared itself nothing even to exhausting and spending itself to give witness to this love; and in recompense, for the most part, I have received only ingratitude," Our Holy Father, in a letter to the Bishop of the Church of Autun, wrote in part: "When I was on a pilgrimage in 1986 to the tomb of Margaret Mary, I asked in the spirit of what has been handed down in the Church that the veneration of the Sacred Heart be faithfully restored. For it is in the Heart of Christ that the human heart learns to know the true and unique meaning of its life and destiny; it is in the Heart of Christ that the human heart receives its capacity to love. In fact, only the Heart of Christ has loved the Father with an undivided love.

"To give to the Sacred Heart of Jesus the place of

veneration due to this Heart in the Church, it is necessary to take up again the exhortation of Saint Paul: 'Have within you the sentiments which were in Christ Jesus' (Philippians 2:15)....

"I encourage pastors, religious communities, and all animators of pilgrimages to Paray-le-Monial to contribute to the diffusion of the message received by Saint Margaret Mary. To you, pastor of the Church of Autun, and to all who will allow themselves to be moved by this teaching, I hope you will discover in the heart of Christ the force of love, the sources of grace, the real presence of the Lord in his Church by the gift daily renewed of His Body and Blood. To each of you, I willingly grant my apostolic blessing."

> Pope John Paul II
> Feast of the Sacred Heart
> June 22, 1990, Vatican

In conclusion, let it be said that Our Holy Father's Angelus Meditations were not without success. By the time he had reached the half-way point in his series of

Sunday Angelus messages, devotion to Christ's Heart was increasing, especially in Brazil. In October 1988, a group of priests, sisters and brothers belonging to congregations with ties to the spirituality of the Sacred Heart of Jesus organized a Congress on this spirituality and its implications for pastoral activities in today's society. Attended by some three hundred religious, it represented sixty religious congregations as well as lay representatives from a dozen dioceses.

The conclusions of the Congress were summed up in a message centered on Communion and fidelity: "Communion with the Son of God who reveals the Trinity's love for all; fidelity to Christ which carries on Christ's mission to the world. This devotion, rooted in biblical revelation and lived in Christian tradition, is encouraged by the teaching Church and animated in faith by the People of God.

II

More recently, on May 31, 1992, His Holiness, Pope John Paul II at the canonization Mass of Saint Claude La Colombière spoke again on the love of the Sacred Heart for the people of God. The main theme of his homily centered around the prayer offered by Christ in the Upper Room to the Apostles the evening before the institution of the Eucharist: "So that your love for me may continue in thom" (Jn 17:26) in the generations to come.

Claude La Colombière, a 17th century Jesuit priest, is known especially for spreading devotion to the Sacred Heart of Jesus. A disciple and spiritual director of St. Margaret Mary, he devoted himself completely in prayer to Christ who revealed to him the secret of His Heart. Through his kinship with St. Margaret Mary at Paray-le-Monial, he was convinced of the authenticity of her mystical experiences. The message she had received from the Lord: "Behold the Heart which has so loved mankind that it spared nothing to exhaust and consume itself in testimony of love," she entrusted to him, "her faithful servant and perfect friend."

Wholeheartedly, Claude La Colombière accepted the mission Margaret Mary passed on to him of establishing "this devotion of giving pleasure to the Divine Heart of Jesus." Convinced that he was the instrument of God's work through the grace that transformed him, Claude began to preach to the faithful the message of "reparation" that God had made known to St. Margaret Mary. This work has had great repercussions in the Church even to our times and has been encouraged by the Vicars of Christ on earth. For example, Pope John Paul II stated the following:

"Pope Leo XIII saw in the Sacred Heart of Jesus a symbol and clear image of Jesus Christ's infinite love, a love which impels us to love one another" (cf. Encyclical Annum sacrum 1900). Pope Pius XI and Pope Pius XII encouraged this devotion and saw in it a spiritual answer to the difficulties which the faith and the Church were facing.

In evangelizing the Church today, His Holiness Pope John Paul II continued in his homily: "The Heart of Christ must be recognized as the heart of the Church; it is He who calls us to conversion, to reconciliation; it is He who leads pure hearts and those hungering for justice along the way of the Beatitudes; it is He who achieves the warm communion of the members of one Body; it is He who enables us to adhere to the Good News and to accept the promise of eternal life; it is He who sends us out on mission. *The Heart to Heart with Jesus broadens the human heart on a global scale.*"

Our Holy Father concluded his homily with this prayer: "May the canonization of Claude La Colombière be for the whole Church an appeal to live the consecration to the Sacred Heart of Jesus, a consecration which is self-giving that allows the charity of Christ to inspire us, pardon us, and lead us in His ardent desire to open the ways of truth and life to all our brothers and sisters."

Thus, through his devotion to the Sacred Heart of Jesus and by his preaching and writings, His Holiness John Paul II has revealed to the Church of our time the legacy of love which Christ gave to the Apostles at the Last Supper in the Upper Room. In the traditions of the Church, this devotion has been transmitted to the people of God throughout the Ages, as Christ willed it, according to the Will of God.

In conclusion, it should be noted that frequently in public celebrations honoring the Sacred Heart of Jesus, the recitation of the Litany is included alternating the invocations and response between the priest presider and the congregation. Hence the Litany of the Sacred Heart of Jesus follows:

LITANY OF THE SACRED HEART

Lord, have mercy on us.
Christ, have mercy on us.
Lord, have mercy on us, Christ, hear us.
Christ, graciously hear us.
God the Father of heaven,
Have mercy on us.
God the Son, Redeemer of the world,
Have mercy on us.
God the Holy Spirit,
Have mercy on us.
Holy Trinity, one God.
Have mercy on us.

1. Heart of Jesus, Son of the eternal Father,
   [After each invocation the response is:
   "Have mercy on us."]
2. Heart of Jesus, formed by the Holy Spirit in the
   womb of the Virgin Mother,
3. Heart of Jesus, substantially united to the Word
   of God,
4. Heart of Jesus, of infinite majesty,
5. Heart of Jesus, sacred temple of God,
6. Heart of Jesus, tabernacle of the Most High,
7. Heart of Jesus, house of God and gate of
   heaven,
8. Heart of Jesus, burning furnace of charity,
9. Heart of Jesus, abode of justice and love,

10. Heart of Jesus, full of goodness and love,
11. Heart of Jesus, abyss of all virtues,
12. Heart of Jesus, most worthy of all praise,
13. Heart of Jesus, king and center of all hearts,
14. Heart of Jesus, in whom are all the treasures of wisdom and knowledge,
15. Heart of Jesus, in whom dwells the fullness of the divinity,
16. Heart of Jesus, in whom the Father was well pleased,
17. Heart of Jesus, of whose fullness we have all received,
18. Heart of Jesus, desire of the everlasting hills,
19. Heart of Jesus, patient and most merciful,
20. Heart of Jesus, enriching all who invoke you,
21. Heart of Jesus, fountain of life and holiness,
22. Heart of Jesus, propitiation for our sins,
23. Heart of Jesus, loaded down with opprobrium,
24. Heart of Jesus, bruised for our offenses,
25. Heart of Jesus, obedient unto death,
26. Heart of Jesus, pierced with a lance,
27. Heart of Jesus, source of all consolation,
28. Heart of Jesus, our life and resurrection,
29. Heart of Jesus, our peace and reconciliation,
30. Heart of Jesus, victim for sin,
31. Heart of Jesus, salvation of those who trust in you,
32. Heart of Jesus, hope of those who die in you,
33. Heart of Jesus, delight of all the saints,

Lamb of God, you take away the sins of the world,
Spare us, Lord.
Lamb of God, you take away the sins of the world,
Graciously hear us, O Lord.
Lamb of God, you take away the sins of the world,
Have mercy on us.
V. Jesus, meek and humble of heart,
R. Make our hearts like unto thine.

Let us pray:

Almighty and eternal God, look upon the Heart of your dearly beloved Son and upon the praise and satisfaction he offers you in the name of sinners, and being appeased, grant pardon to those who seek your mercy, in the name of the same Jesus Christ, your Son, who lives and reigns with you in the unity of the Holy Spirit, world without end. Amen.

*　　*　　*

Biographical Sketch

SISTER MARIE CELESTE, S.C.

Sister Marie Celeste, SC is a Mother Seton Sister of Charity, a professor of Modern Languages and Literatures, and an international scholar and author. She holds a PhD in French Studies from Laval University, Quebec, certificates of study from the Sorbonne and *L'Institut Catholique* of Paris, from the University of Madrid, and from the University of Perugia, Italy. Her books and translations have been published in France, Canada and the United States. Her major French works embody studies on Georges Bernanos, Graham Greene and the famed Black-African author, Cheikh Hamidou Kane. An official biographer of Elizabeth Ann Bayley Seton, she has authored several major works based on the saint's own writings, namely, *A Self-Portrait; The Intimate Friendships; A Woman of Prayer.* She has won numerous awards in the United States and abroad and is listed in the *World's Who's Who of Women.*